THE CHILDREN'S ILLUSTRATED ATLAS OF THE WORLD

Molly Perham and Philip Steele

CONTENTS

TEMPLAR

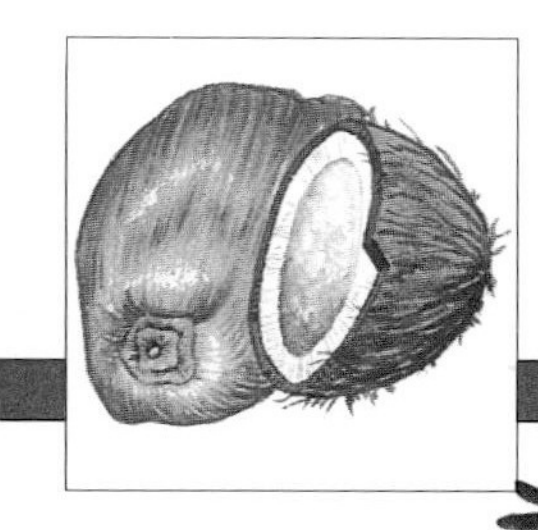

THE EARTH and how this atlas works

Maps are used to show what the Earth looks like on a flat piece of paper. This is helpful if you want to find out where a new place is or understand where you are in relation to other people and places. Maps are a good way of communicating information about the world.

In this section of the atlas you will find out how mapmakers draw the shape of things and use lines, symbols and color to give a useful picture of the Earth's surface.

In the main part of the atlas you will discover the great variety of landscapes that can be found in the world. From vast, flat plains to great mountain ranges; from countries with mighty rivers and forests to those usually covered in ice.

The back of the book contains a useful reference source of important facts about each country, and a gazetteer to tell you where you can find a particular place in the atlas.

How to find your position on the Earth

One of the most important jobs a map can do is to tell you the position of a particular place. You may wish to know where a friend lives or how far you need to travel to visit a new place.

The Earth is a spherical, or ball-like, shape with an enormous area. Land and sea combined, the surface area of the world is 196,800,00 square miles; sea covers about 70 percent of its surface. The distance around the middle of the Earth – the circumferences at the Equator – is 24,901,55 miles.

To find your way around this vast area you need a system of fixed reference points from which distances can be measured. A network of imaginary lines is drawn on the globe to provide these reference points. These lines are known as latitude and longitude.

Latitude

Lines of Latitude are imaginary lines drawn around the world from east to west. The line drawn around the center of the world is numbered 0 and is called the Equator. As you move further away from the Equator to the north the numbers increase up to 90° N, which is the North Pole. The numbers also increase as you move south of the Equator up to 90° S, which is the South Pole.

Latitude tells you how far north or south of the Equator you are. The lines, also called parallels, are measured in degrees. One degree of latitude is about 70 miles. Each degree if further divided into 60 minutes. At 23° 27' N of the Equator lies the Tropic of Cancer, and at the same distance south lies the Tropic of Capricorn. These two lines mark the most northerly and southerly places where the sun ever shines directly overhead.

Longitude

Lines, or meridians, of longitude, are drawn around the globe from north to south. They join the North Pole to the South Pole. The line of longitude that passes through Greenwich, London, England is numbered 0 and is called the Prime Meridian or the Greenwich Meridian.

As you move east or west away from the Prime Meridian, the numbers increase up to the 180 meridian which is in the Pacific Ocean. All the meridians of longitude meet at the North and South Poles. The distance between the meridians is greatest at the Equator and decrease as the lines get nearer the Poles.

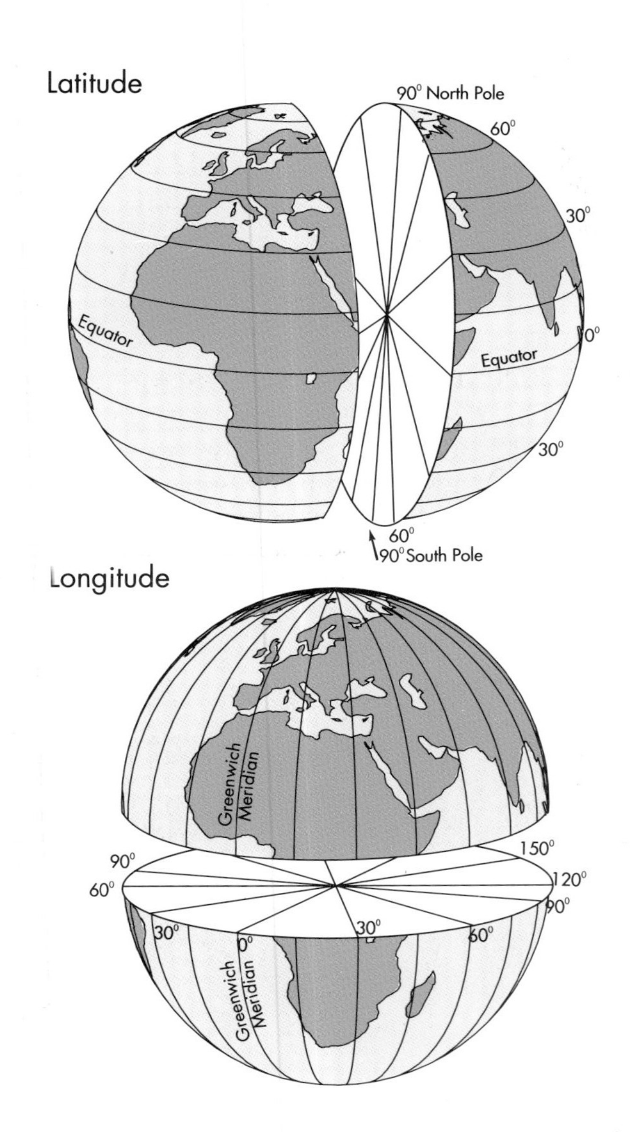

GRIDS and GRATICULES

The network of the graticule

The combination of the lines of latitude and longitude produces a network or grid of imaginary lines that is known as the graticule. Any place on the globe can be pinpointed exactly using these two lines. The latitude of the place is always given first as degrees and minutes north or south of the Equator, followed by the longitude as degrees and minutes east or west of the Greenwich Meridian.

In the map below the latitude of Istanbul is 41° 02' N and the longitude is 29° 00' E.

Using a grid reference

Except for the political maps, all the maps in this atlas have a simplified graticule of straight grid lines with numbers and letters around the edge. These grid lines can be used to find places on that map. In the gazetteer, the alphabetical list of towns, cities, rivers, mountains and islands has a page number followed by a letter and a number. If you turn to the correct page, the letter and number will show you in which square you will find the feature you are looking for. In the map below the grid reference of Istanbul is A1.

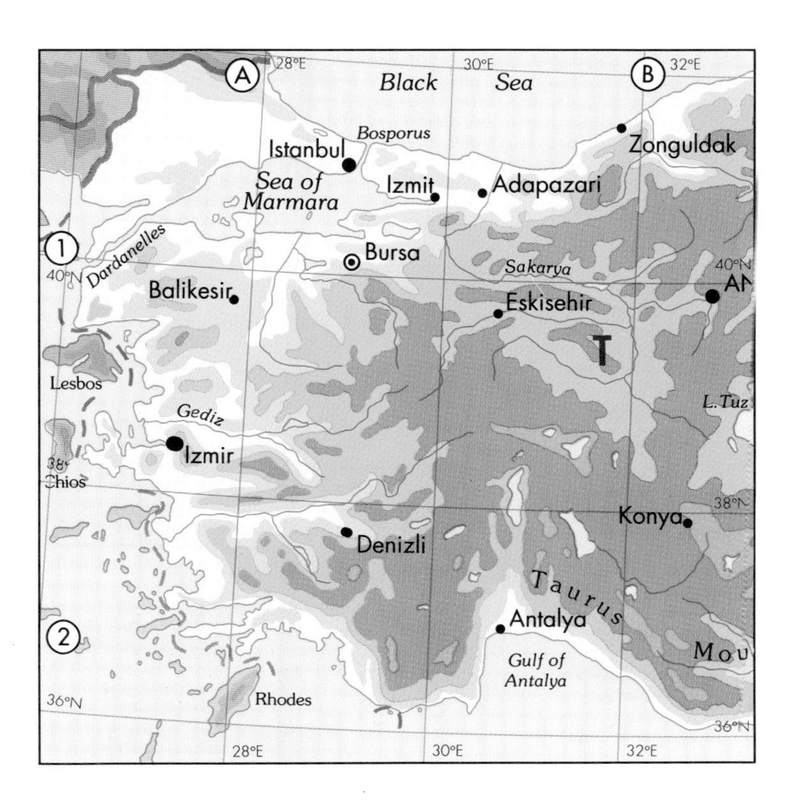

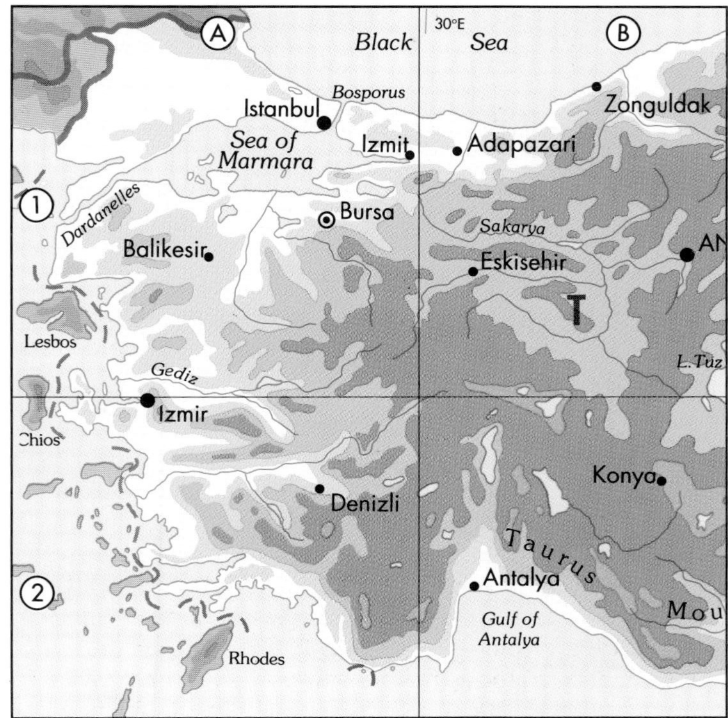

Transferring detail from the spherical earth....

Because the Earth is spherical the only way to represent its features accurately is on a globe. A cartographer, a person who draws maps, has to solve the problem of representing the curved globe on a flat piece of paper.

If the Earth could be peeled like an orange and the skin, with all the detail printed on it, was laid flat, great tears would appear as you can see below. These tears make it impossible to show the distances, directions and areas of a spherical Earth on a flat piece of paper without having either gaping holes or distortion.

Over the page you can see the different ways maps can be drawn to overcome this problem.

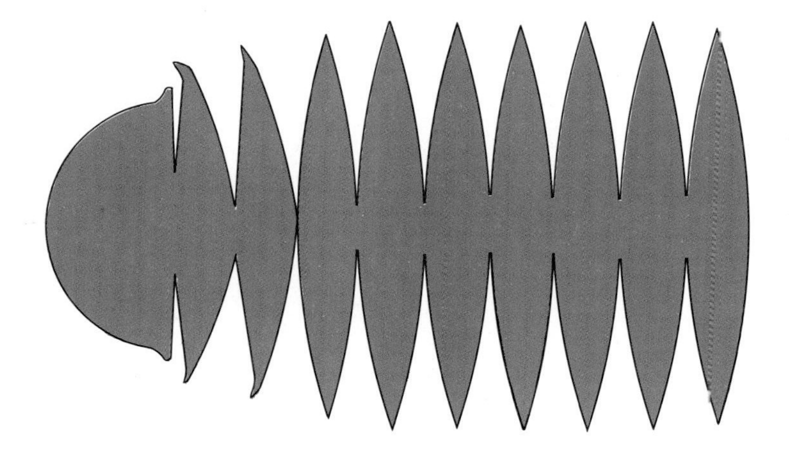

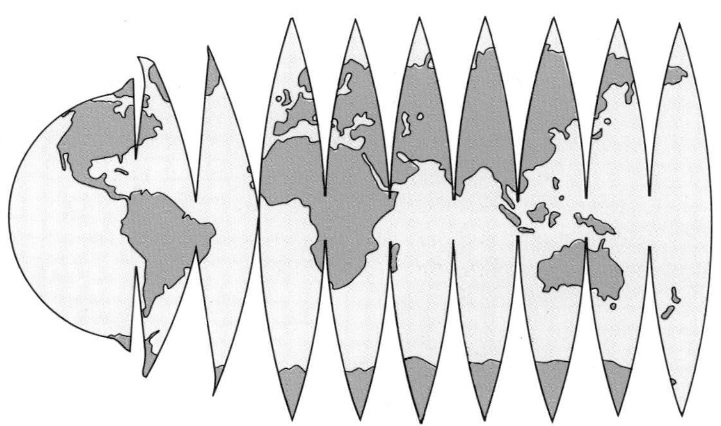

....to a flat piece of paper

MAP PROJECTIONS

When cartographers transfer details from the globe onto a flat map they use the graticule as a framework. The system of transferring the graticule is known as map projection.

It is impossible to project the graticule accurately on a flat map, as it has to be shrunk in some places and stretched in others. So all maps show some distortion. The choice of projection depends on the subject and use of the map and the geographical area it covers.

Three different kinds of projections are shown below.

Azimuthal projections

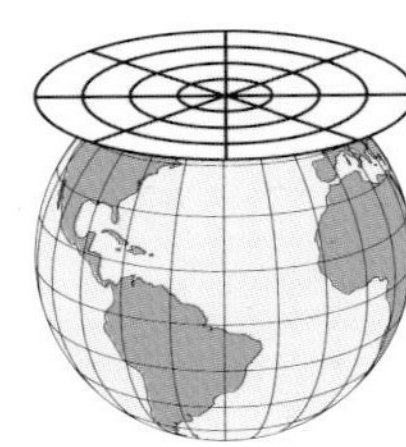

Azimuthal projections project part of the globe onto a flat surface. Imagine that a piece of paper just touches the globe at one point. If a light is shone through the globe then the shadow made by the graticule on the paper would be an azimuthal projection. The point where the paper touches the globe would be totally free from distortion, but a distortion of both shape and scale would occur as you move away from the center. Azimuthal projections are used for mapping areas such as the poles.

Lambert's Azimuthal Projection

Conical projections

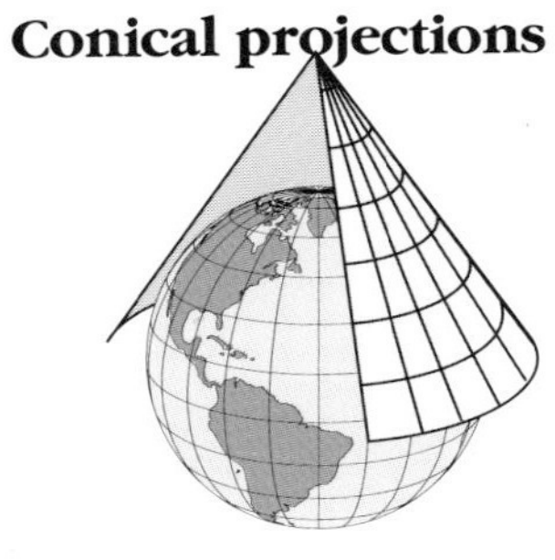

Conical projections are produced by transferring the lines of latitude and longitude from the globe onto a cone. The cone can be positioned on the globe along one parallel of latitude and the line where the paper rests on the globe will have no distortion, but as you move away from that line, distortion will increase. Conic projections are useful for middle-latitude countries, especially those with a large east–west extent such as the United States of America.

Albers Conic Projection

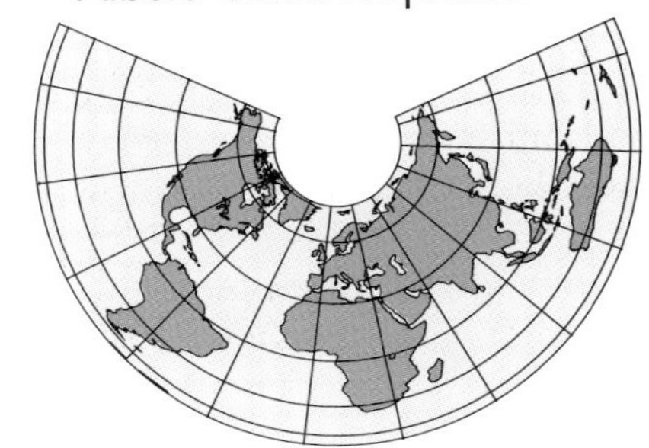

Cylindrical projections

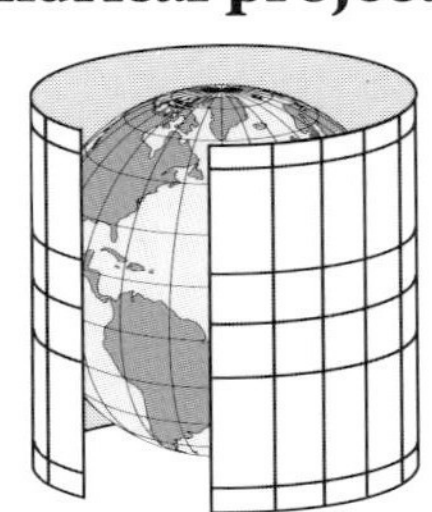

If a cylinder of paper is wrapped around a globe, the resulting map will have only one line that is free from distortion – the Equator. But, because lines of longitude do not touch at the poles, as you get further away from the Equator into the high-latitude areas the lines are stretched and distorted considerably. This type of projection is usually used for world maps. Mercator's projection is one of the best known examples.

Mercator Projection

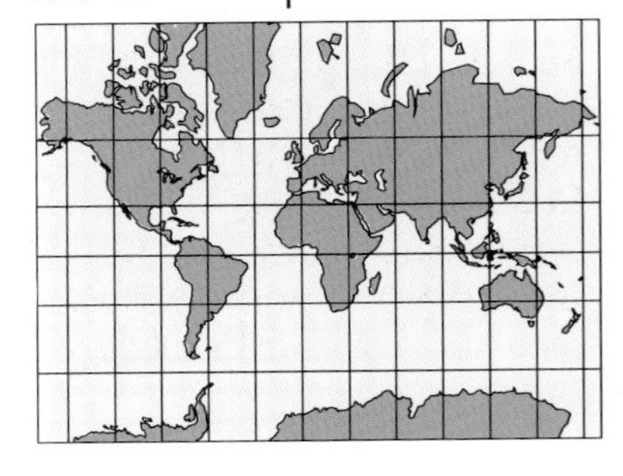

Three projections of Australia

Mapmakers choose the projection according to the use of the map. They consider such things as the shape of areas, directions and distances. See how different the shape of Australia is in these three different projections.

Lambert's Azimuthal Projection

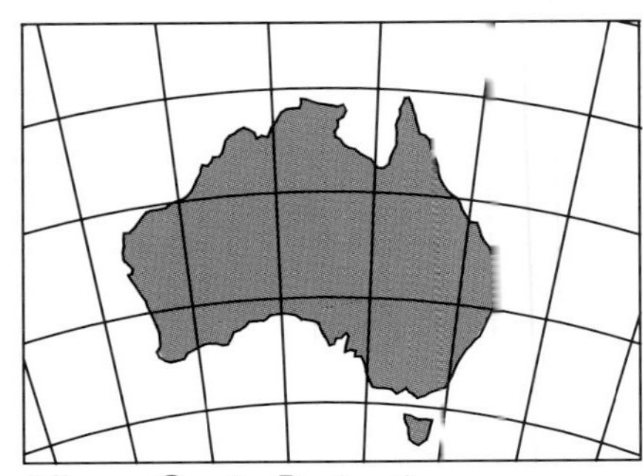

Albers Conic Projection

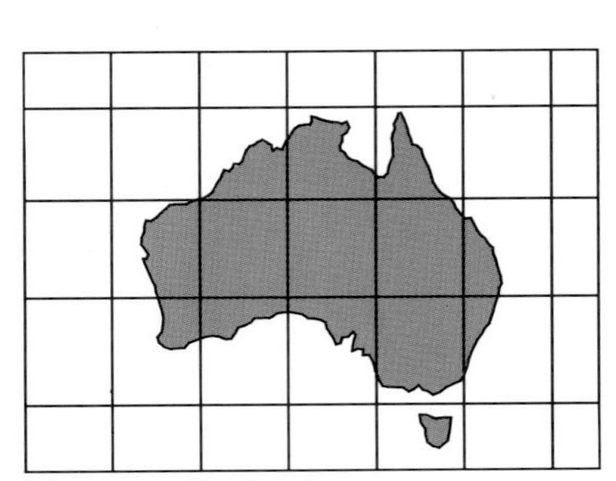

Mercator Projection

SCALES and SYMBOLS

Scales

To be of any use, maps have to reduce or scale-down what they represent. Scale is the ratio between the distance on the map and the distance on the ground. A map the same size as the object being drawn is known as a one to one, that is it is drawn at a 1:1 scale. The scale is only useful for really detailed engineering drawings of small objects.

If the scale is 1:1,000,000 then one inch of map represents 1,000,000 inches (15.8 miles) on the ground. If the scale is 1:30,000,000 one inch now represents 30,000,000 inches (473.5 miles). The scale becomes smaller as the number of inches gets bigger.

Maps and Scales

For the purposes of mapping our surroundings, the largest scale normally used would be 1:1,000 (one to one thousand). At this scale the streets around your house, the sidewalk and even the shed in the backyard could be shown accurately. These large-scale maps are usually produced by the official mapping organization of a country. From these maps, others are drawn at smaller scales.

Smaller scale maps can show a larger area of a country on the same size of paper. At a scale of 1:1,000 the area shown on a map may only be about 55,562 square yards (0.17 square miles); at a scale of 1:20,000 the area covered would be 22,152,300 square yards (7.1 square miles). If the scale is reduced further still to 1:100,000, then 55,440,650 square yards (178.7 square miles) can be shown

Whenever you use a map, the scale is one of the first things to look for. It is usually printed somewhere at the edge of the map. Most of the maps in this atlas have scales between 1:5,000,000 and 1:40,000,000. At these scales whole countries can be shown on a page.

A scale bar, a horizontal line divided into sections, is another way of showing the scale of a map. If you take a ruler and measure a distance on the map you can then work out the exact distance in real life using the scale bar.

Using different scales

The maps on the right show the same city, Bombay, but at different scales. Map 1 is the largest scale and Map 3 the smallest.

In Map 1, the roads in Bombay can be shown. You can measure these roads by using the scale bar.

In Map 2, Bombay is shown by a spot. You can measure how far Bombay is from nearby towns by using the scale bar.

In Map 3, the position of Bombay within India can be seen. You can measure how far Bombay is from the other side of India by using the scale bar.

Map 1

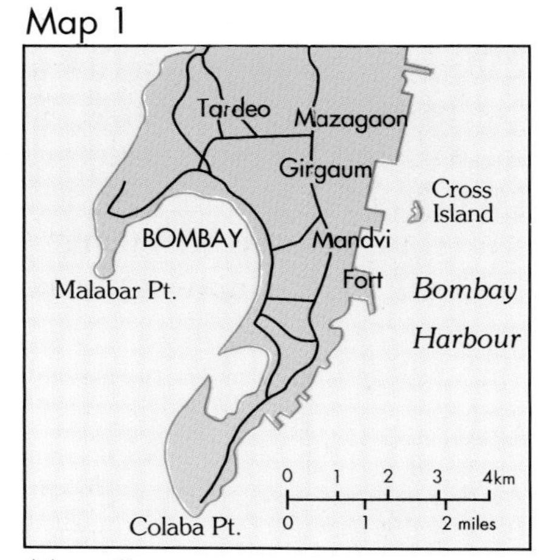

Map 2

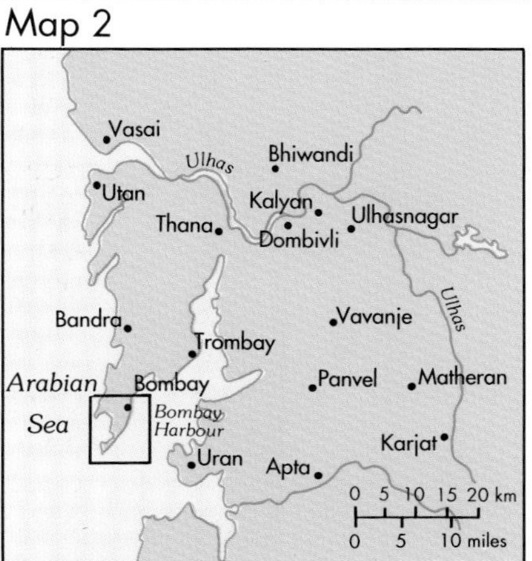

Map 3

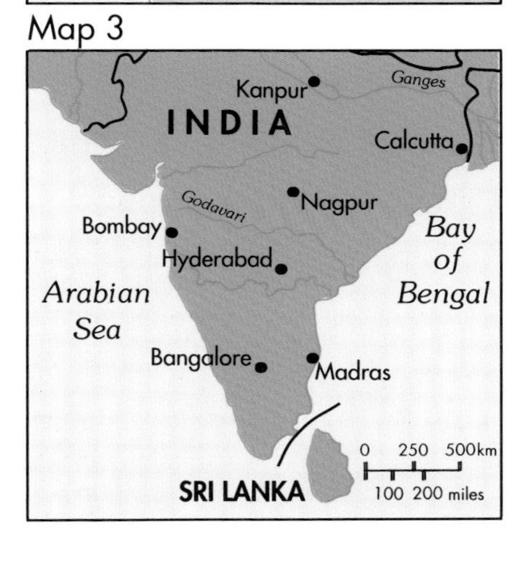

Symbols

Symbols are used on maps to represent features on the ground. They are not usually drawn to scale and may often be exaggerated in size in order to show something that is important. Three main types of symbols are used on maps. Point symbols show such features as mountain peaks, towns, airports and waterfalls. Line symbols show such features as international boundaries, roads, rivers and railways. Area symbols show such features as natural vegetation and land use.

The symbols used in this atlas are shown on pages 12-13. The various symbols shown below are examples of symbols used in other atlases, maps and tourist guides.

Point Symbols		Line Symbols		Area Symbols
● town	⋀ campsite	▬ ▬ ▬ boundary	——— railway	desert
★ capital city	swimming pool	river	═══ motorway	forest
church with tower	tourist information	canal	= = = minor road	swamp

WHAT MAPS CAN SHOW

Maps can be used to show all sorts of different information. Most of the maps in this atlas are general reference maps. They show a mix of physical geography, the natural features of the land, and human geography, which is the effect that man has on the land. The natural features shown include coastlines, rivers and the height of the land. Man-made features include international boundaries, towns and cities.

Color or contour lines can be added to maps to show the height of the land. A contour line is used to join places of the same height and can create bands of color. If the color changes quickly or the contour lines are closer together it shows that the land in that area is rising steeply.

The following maps show how different types of information can be given in many different ways.

Different views of the world

Most world maps show the North Pole at the top of the page and the land masses as the most important features. But if we look at the four views of the world, shown below as globes, we can see just how much water there is compared to land. Each view gives us different information about land and ocean masses.

Western

Eastern

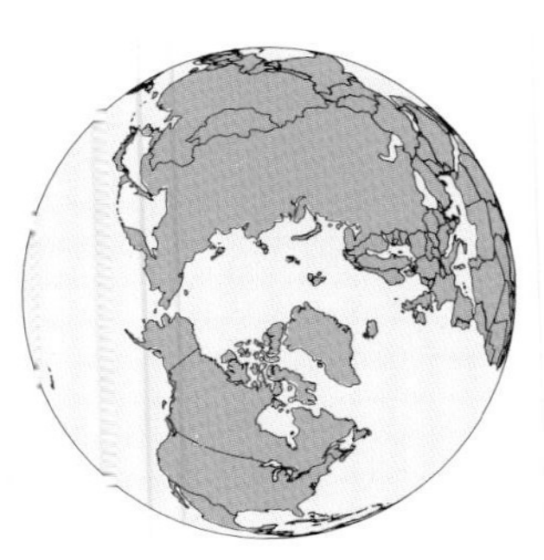

Northern

Southern

World population by country

Sometimes information can be shown more clearly by replacing the physical contours of a map with colors or lines. In the map below, the real coastline and area of each country have been replaced by squares that represent the total population of that country. This is a good map for comparing the populations of countries at a glance. Different colors are used to show the population density of each country. In this atlas population density is given as the average number of people per square kilometer.

Road distance map of France

The natural road pattern of some road maps can also be replaced by straight lines. For example, if you look at these road maps of France, the one on the left is how we normally see a road map. The map on the right, however, shows the roads of France as straight lines so the distances can be measured easily. This, however, means that the towns, for example Nice, are not always in their correct geographical position.

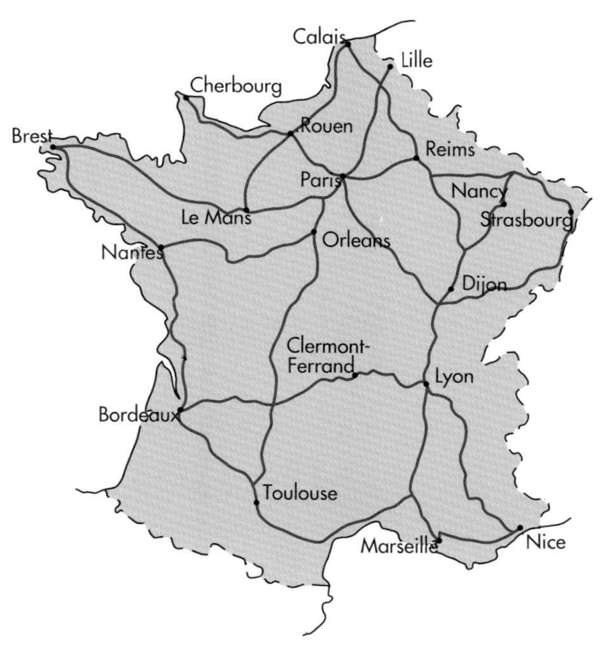

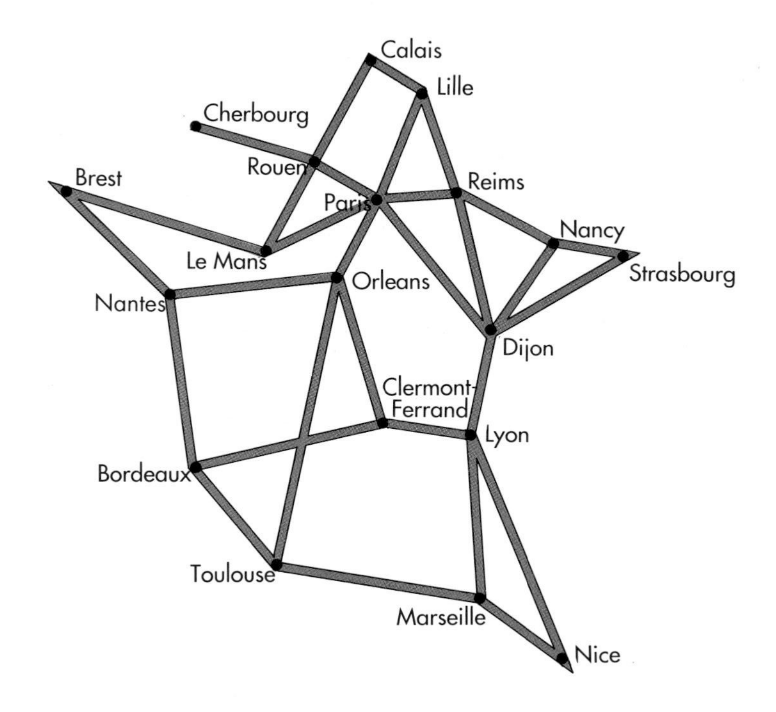

World production of metals

Thematic maps, which show the distribution of various factors, retain their normal physical appearance. The map below, for example, shows where different metals in the world can be found. Symbols are used to locate these metals. The background colors show which countries produce the most metals. From the map you can compare metal production in Canada and Australia. Other thematic maps are shown on the next page.

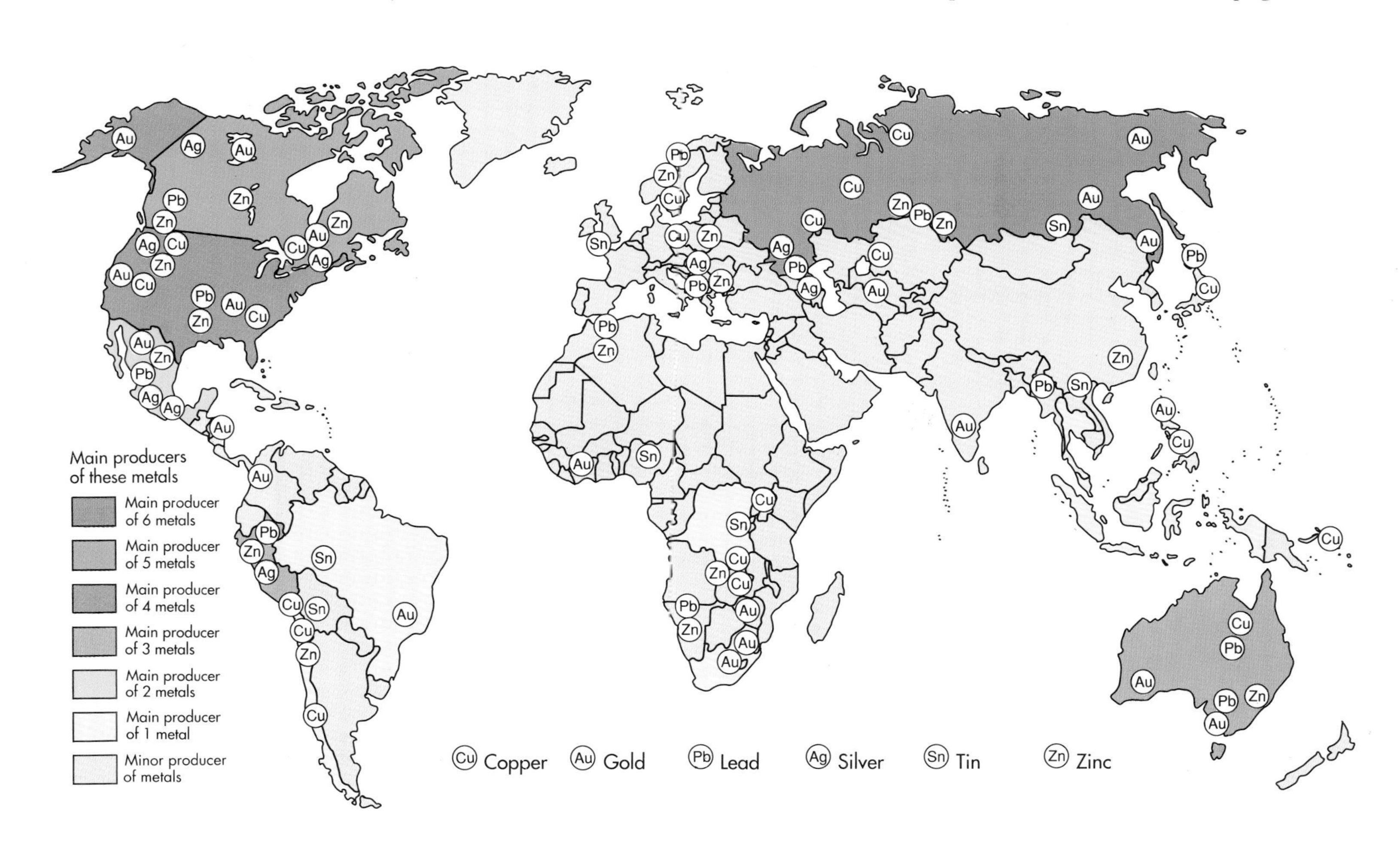

WORLD THEMATIC MAPS

World temperatures: January

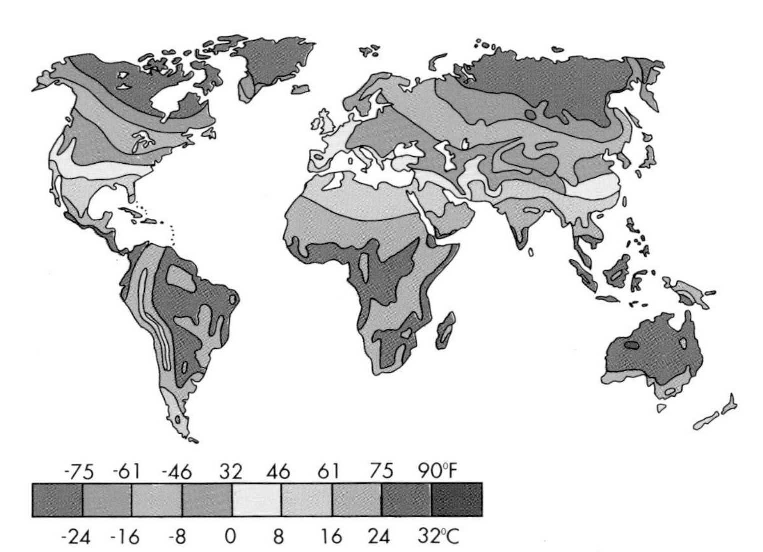

The highest temperature ever recorded was at Al Aziziyah, Libya on September 13 1922 136°F

World temperatures: July

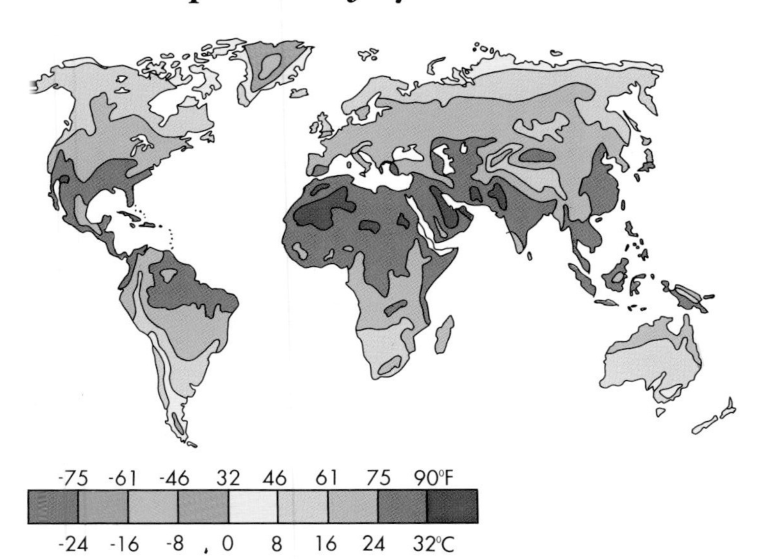

The lowest temperature ever recorded was at Vostok, Antarctica on July 21 1983 -129°F

Annual World Rainfall

Mt. Waialeale, Hawaii, has the highest amount of rain every year – 460 inches
Arica, Chile, has the lowest amount of rainfall every year – .3 inches

World Earthquake and Volcano Zones

World Religions

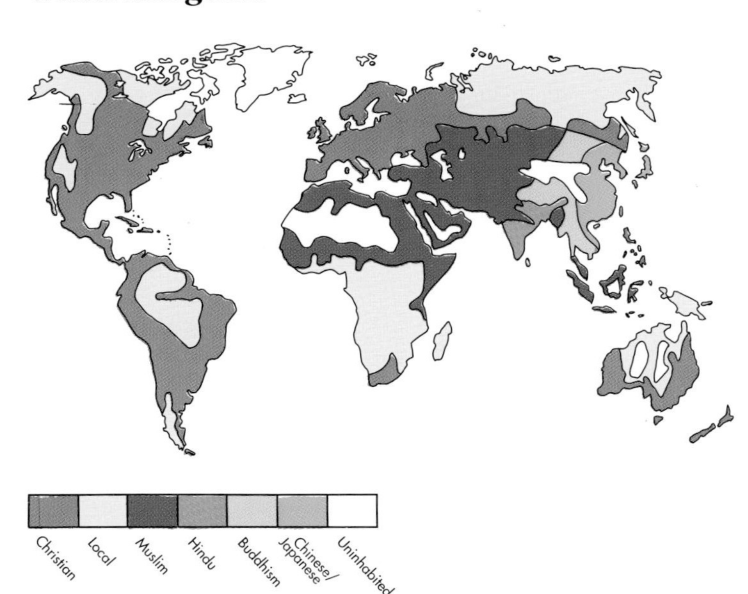

World Languages

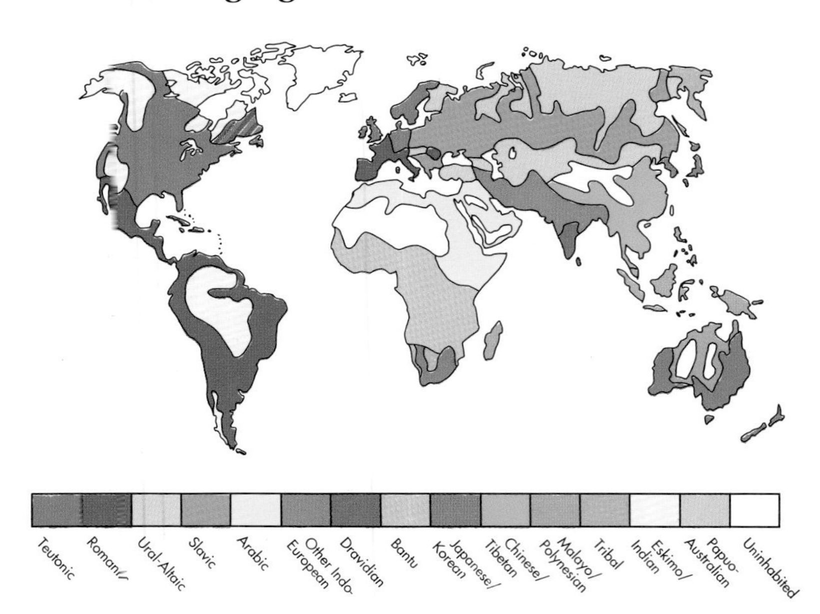

GLOSSARY

Some words in this atlas may be new to you. A brief explanation for these is given below.

Atoll A ring-shaped coral reef enclosing an area of shallow water called a lagoon.

Cash crops Crops grown mainly for sale and not for the farmer's own use. Cash crops include food crops such as wheat, and crops such as rubber and sugar cane that have to be processed before use.

Climate The average weather conditions of a place over a number of years.

Coral Coral is made up of millions of tiny creatures that live in shallow tropical seas. When these animals die, their chalky skeletons form coral reefs, atolls, and islands.

Continental Shelf A sloping platform of land around the continents covered by relatively shallow water. Outside this shelf, the ocean bed descends steeply.

Crust The outer layer of the Earth.

Deep-sea ridges and trenches Ranges of hills and deep valleys on the ocean floor.

Delta Deltas, triangular shaped areas of sand, gravel, and silt, form at the mouth of rivers because the sand and mud carried down the river are not swept away by sea currents.

Dyke A bank or wall to hold back floodwater or the sea. It can also be a ditch for draining the land.

Earthquake A sudden movement of the rocks within the Earth's crust produces shock waves which shake the surface of the Earth.

EC The European Community was first established as the European Economic Community or Common Market in 1957. The original member-ship of 6 (Belgium, France, Italy, Luxembourg, Netherlands, West Germany) has grown to include most states in Western Europe.

Glacier A mass of ice which slowly moves downhill, often along a river valley which it deepens and straightens.

Hurricane A severe tropical storm with spiraling winds that move at great speeds and do a great deal of damage. In the Pacific Ocean, similar storms are called typhoons; in the Indian Oceans they are called cyclones.

Hydroelectric power The electric power generated as water from a waterfall, dam, or pipeline passes through turbine machines in a power station.

Ice Ages Periods in the Earth's history when ice sheets spread over areas of the world which now have a warmer climate. The largest ice sheet today covers Antarctica.

Minerals Naturally occurring substances such as diamonds and metal ores which can be extracted from the ground by mining.

Mixed economy Countries with mixed economies make their money from a number of different industries. Some of these industries are owned by the state; others are privately owned.

Monsoon A monsoon is a wind that brings torrential rain to an area causing a wet season. Some areas in Asia have two monsoons a year; others have just one.

Oasis An area in a desert where water is available at or near the surface of the ground. Some oases are small and can only support a few plants and animals; others support thriving towns.

Pampas Vast, treeless grassy plains of South America, south of the River Amazon.

Peninsula An area of land almost surrounded by water but still attached to the mainland.

Plain A lowland area with a fairly level surface, though there may be hills in some areas.

Plantation A large farm on which only one main cash crop is grown, e.g. tea and coffee plantations.

Plate The surface of the Earth is made up of a series of rigid but movable plates of rock called the lithosphere.

Plateau An upland area with a fairly level surface. However, plateaus may have hills and be divided by deep valleys.

Prairie Large, usually treeless, areas of flat grassland especially in North America.

Reef A ridge of coral, rock, shingle, or sand at, or just above or below, the surface of the water.

Savanna Hot, tropical grassland, especially in Africa, where there are two seasons – a wet and a dry.

Staple food The main, basic foods on which a country relies to feed its people.

Steppe Vast, often treeless, grassy plains found in cooler areas such as Siberia.

Strait A narrow passage of water connecting two seas or large areas of water.

Taiga Pine forests that grow between the tundra and steppe.

Tundra A treeless area around the Arctic circle where only lichens and small plants can survive.

Volcano A cone of rock through which molten rock, called lava, escapes from deep in the earth under great pressure.

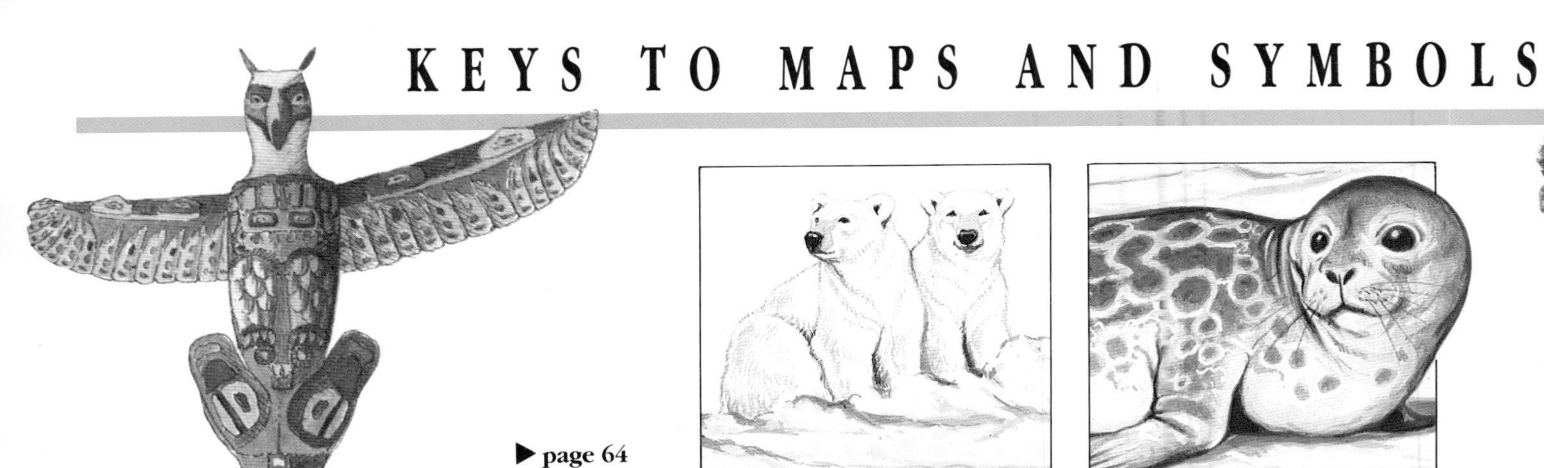

▲ page 52

▶ page 64

▶ page 21

▲ page 54

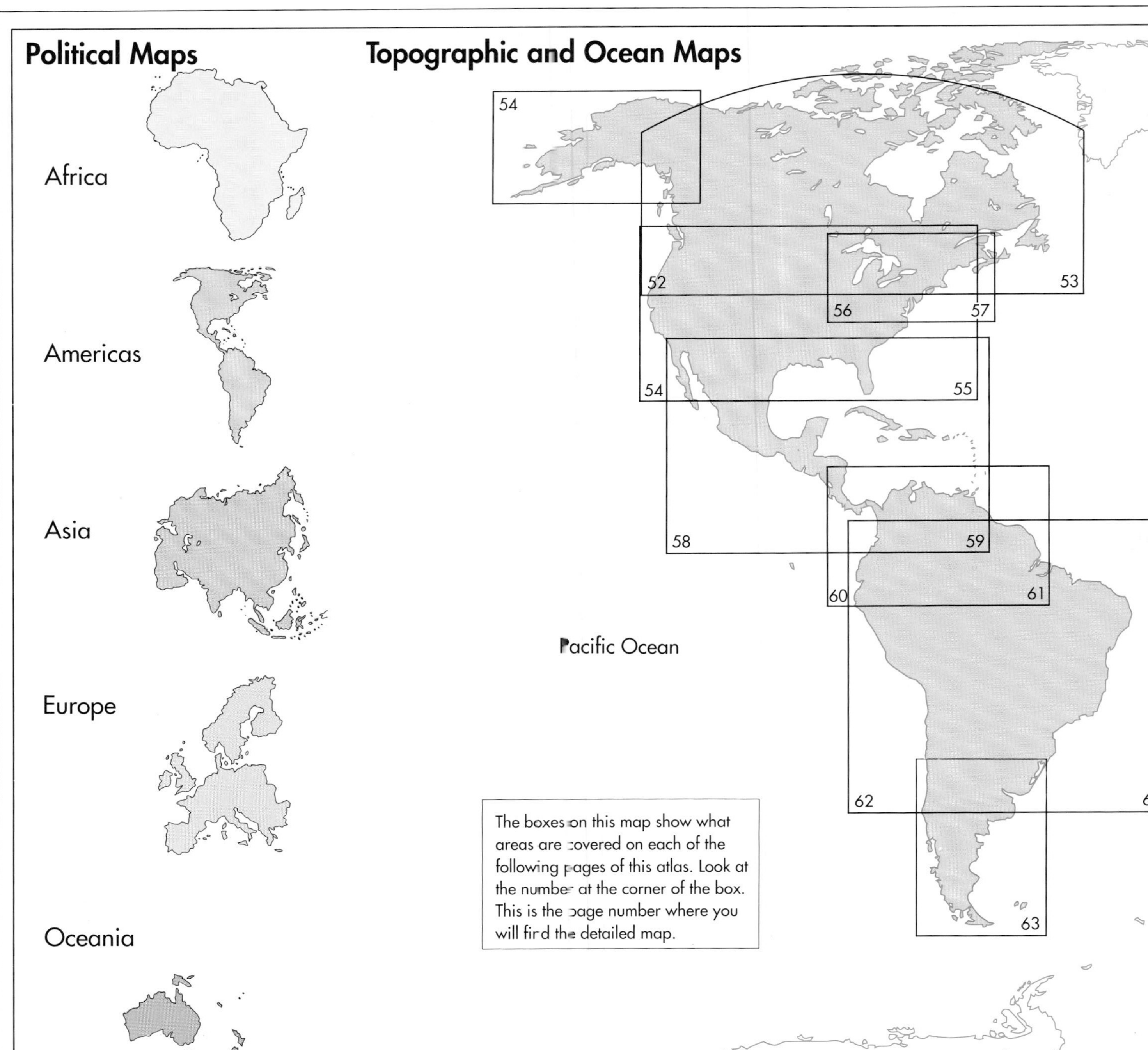

▲ page 61

Colors, symbols and lettering used in this atlas

Country name	AUSTRALIA
Dependency	French Guiana
Possession	(Ecuador)
State or province	QUEENSLAND
Capital city	WELLINGTON
Other city or town	Auckland
Land feature	Nubian Desert C. Agulhas
Water feature	*L. Taupo* *Volga*

- International boundary
- International boundary, undefined or disputed
- International boundary, at sea
- State or province boundary
- State or province boundary, at sea
- Equator
- Tropic or polar circle

Towns and cities:-population size

More than 1,000,000 people	●
Between 500,000 and 1,000,000 people	⊙
Between 100,000 and 500,000 people	•
Less than 100,000 people	○

Physical features:-

Mountain peak	▲ Mt. Everest 8,848 m
Depression on land	▼ Qattara Depression - 133 m
Depth at sea	· Challenger Deep - 10,915 m

▲ page 63

◀▲ page 30
page 34
page 39

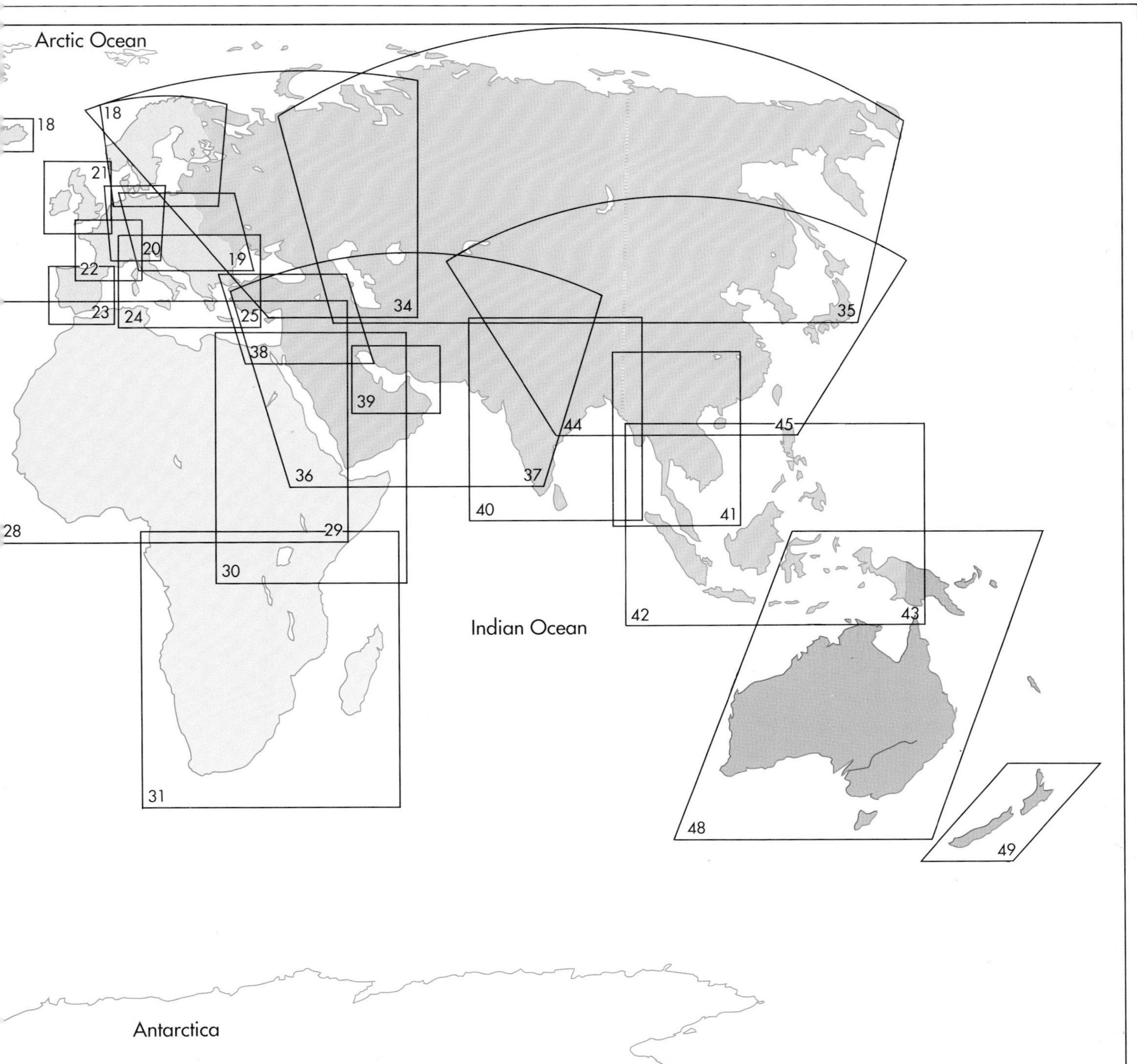

▲ page 41

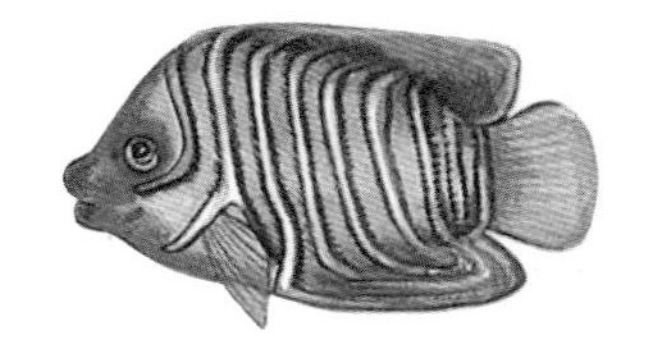
▲ page 66

▲ page 44

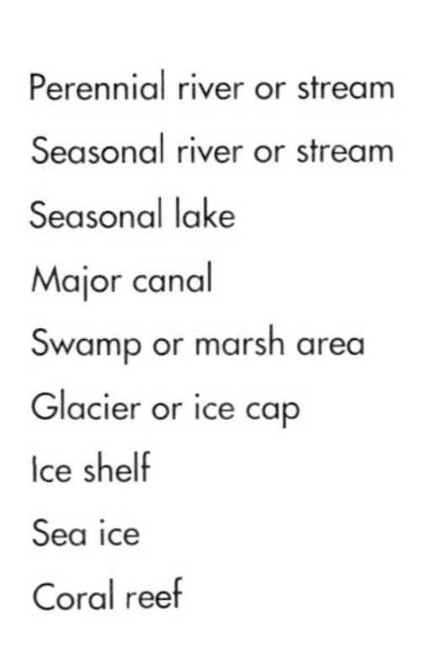

Colors showing the height of the land

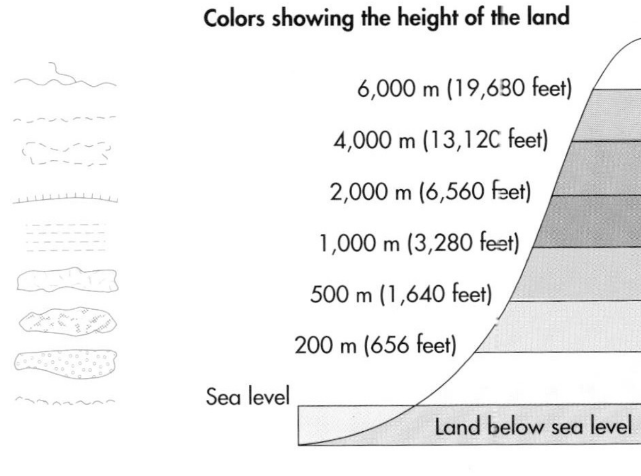

Colors showing the depth of the sea

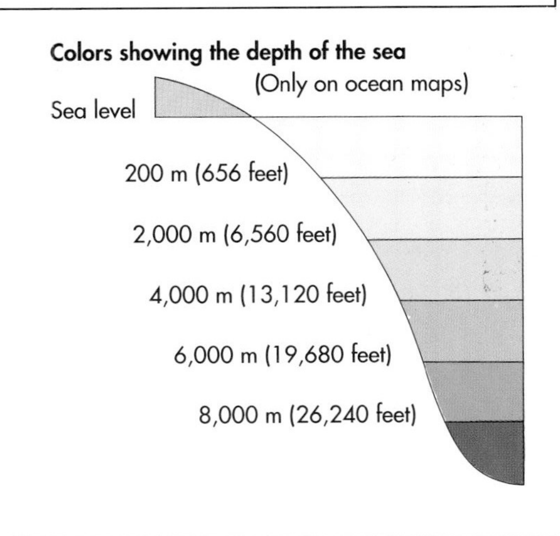

▼ page 48

THE WORLD

Different types of climate and vegetation divide the world into distinct natural regions. The polar regions are always cold and mainly dry, so that few plants can survive. Temperate climates range from the hot, dry summers and mild winters of the Mediterranean to the cooler, wetter climates of Northern Europe. Plants and animals have adapted to the seasonal changes. Tropical zones are wet and warm with abundant vegetation.

Polar Tundra
In the polar tundra of Alaska, northern Canada, and Siberia, the ground is frozen for much of the year. Only lichens, mosses, and small plants can survive. These flower in the short summer (see right).

Woodland and Meadows
Deciduous forests once covered most of the cool, temperate regions. The trees were felled to provide farming and building land. In parts only woodland and meadows remain (see above).

Tropical Savanna
Between the tropical rain forest and desert regions lie large stretches of grassland called savanna. There is a wet, rainy season, followed by periods of drought.

Deserts
Deserts cover over a quarter of the land surface. Some are hot and sandy; others are cold and rocky. All have very little rain and few plants grow.

Rain Forests
Countries close to the Equator have a hot climate and heavy rainfall all year. Trees and plants grow quickly and provide habitats for a rich variety of animal life.

Nations of the World

The countries shown on this world political map are shown in greater detail on the page number given. Key facts can be found on pages 70 – 74

Afghanistan	36/37	Barbados	58/59	Burma (Myanmar)	41	Congo	31	Estonia	34	Guinea Bissau	28/29	Jama
Albania	24/25	Belorus	34	Burundi	30	Costa Rica	58/59	Ethiopia	30	Guyana	60/61	Japa
Algeria	28/29	Belgium	20	Cambodia		Croatia	24/25	Fiji	46/47	Haiti	58/59	Jorda
Andorra	23	Belize	58/59	(Kampuchea)	41	Cuba	58/59	Finland	18	Honduras	58/59	Kazak
Angola	31	Benin	28/29	Cameroon	28/29	Cyprus	38	France	22	Hungary	19	Keny
Antigua & Barbuda	58/59	Bhutan	40	Canada	52/53	Denmark	18	Gabon	31	Iceland	18	Kirgh
Argentina	62/63	Bolivia	62/63	Cape Verde	26/27	Djibouti	30	Gambia, The	28/29	India	40	Kiriba
Armenia	34	Bosnia &		Central African		Dominica	58/59	Georgia	34	Indonesia	42/43	Korea
Australia	48	Hercegovina	24/25	Republic	28/29	Dominican Republic	58/59	Germany	20	Iran	36/37	Korea
Austria	19	Botswana	31	Chad	28/29	Ecuador	60/61	Ghana	28/29	Iraq	36/37	Kuwa
Azerbaijan	34	Brazil	62/63	Chile	62/63	Egypt	30	Greece	24/25	Ireland	21	Laos
Bahamas	58/59	Brunei	42/43	China	44/45	El Salvador	58/59	Grenada	58/59	Israel	38	Latvia
Bahrain	36/37	Bulgaria	24/25	Colombia	60/61	Equatorial Guinea	31	Guatemala	58/59	Italy	24/25	Lebar
Bangladesh	40	Burkina Faso	28/29	Comoros	31	Eritrea	30	Guinea	28/29	Ivory Coast	28/29	Lesot

Coniferous Forest

The vast coniferous forest that stretches round the northern hemisphere is called the taiga. Evergreen trees such as spruce, pine, fir, and larch are able to grow there (see right). The boundary between the taiga and the tundra is known as the tree line.

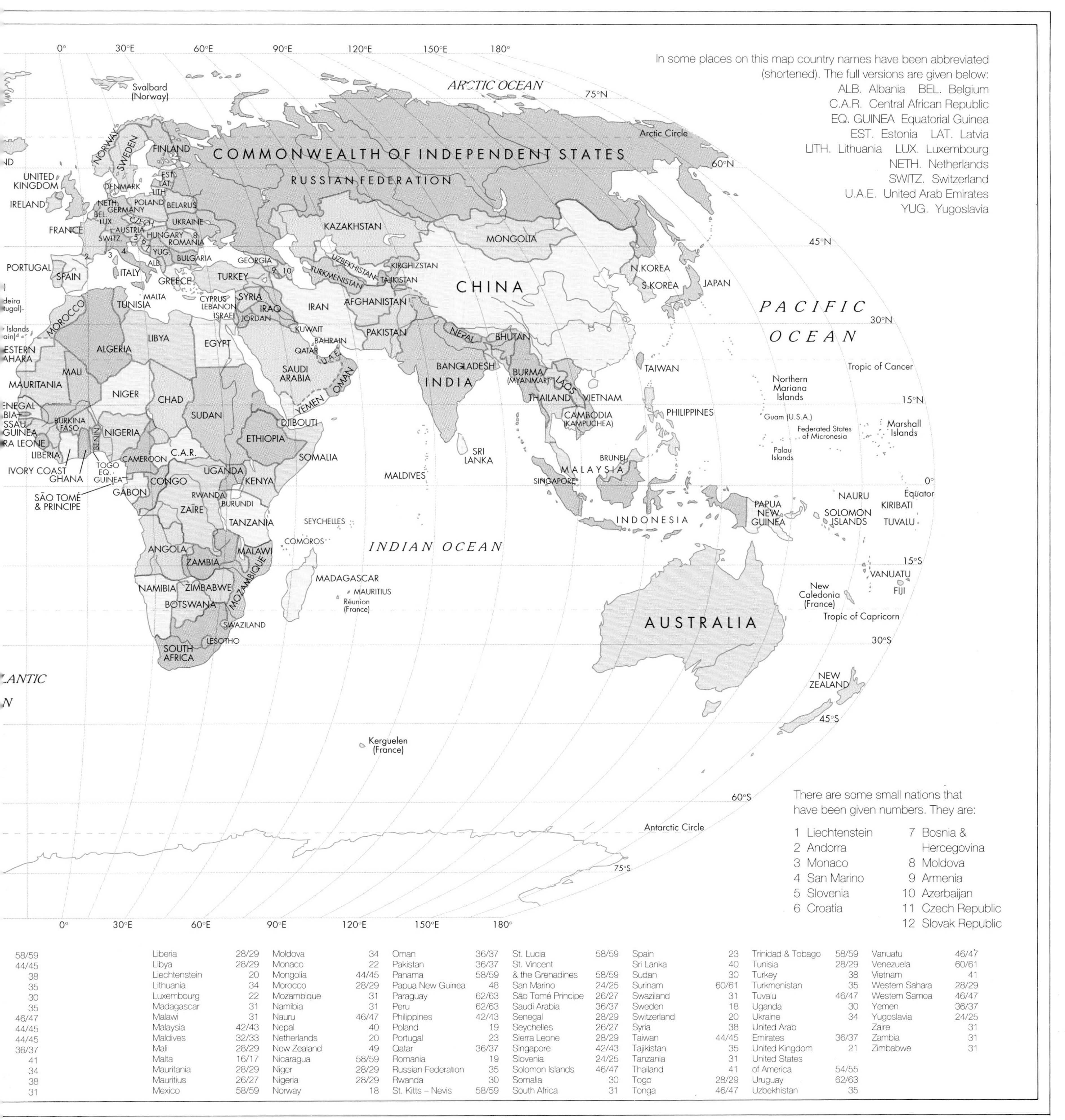

EUROPE

A Cosmopolitan Society
Europeans have diverse origins, so their coloring and appearance are varied. Nordic people are fair, while most Mediterraneans are dark. Immigrants from Africa, Asia, and other countries make up a cosmopolitan society.

Europe is the smallest continent of the northern hemisphere. The Ural Mountains form a boundary with Asia to the east, and on the other three sides it is surrounded by sea. The coastline is 50,000 miles long, so nowhere in western Europe is far from a port. This has encouraged fishing and provided a cheap and easy way of carrying goods from one place to another.

Europe has many natural advantages. It is rich in coal and iron, there is a temperate climate, and a greater proportion of the land can be farmed than in any other continent.

Scale approximately 1:17,200,000

0 200 400 600 km
0 100 200 300 miles

Industrial Wealth
Much of Europe's wealth comes from factories and mines. Britain, northern France, Belgium, and Germany are the principal manufacturing centers. They depend on their deposits of iron, coal, oil, and natural gas.

Food for all Seasons

Although Europe is intensively farmed, it cannot produce enough food for its vast population.

Grain, sugar beet, and potatoes are the main crops in the north and east. Wetter regions to the west provide pasture for dairy cattle. The mild climate of the south produces vines, olives, and citrus fruit.

A Land of Trees

An enormous variety of tree species grow throughout Europe. Evergreen conifers include pine, spruce, and fir trees (see left), while broadleaved trees that shed their leaves in autumn include oak, beech, and chestnut (see below).

Population

Europe has a large population of around 690 million. Some countries are much more densely populated than others. In Norway, Sweden, and Finland, there are wide stretches of almost useless land where no one lives because the ground is not fit for cultivation. These three countries together, though four times the size of the British Isles, have only a quarter as many people.

Number of people per square kilometer

- more than 100
- 10-100
- 2-10
- less than 2

FACT CHART

- The first six countries to join together in 1957 as a European Community were Belgium, Italy, France, Luxembourg, West Germany, and the Netherlands.
- Europe covers only one-thirtieth of the land in the world, but about one-eighth of the world's people live there.
- Mont Blanc is the highest mountain in the Alps and the second highest in Europe after Mount Elbruz (18,510 feet) in the Caucasus. It has several peaks, one of which rises to 15,771 feet. On the northwestern slopes there are numerous glaciers.
- In the Ice Ages much of Europe was covered with vast sheets of ice. The last Ice Age ended about 20,000 years ago. During that time ice sheets spread over an area of about 17 million square miles.
- Between the mountains of the north and south lies the North European Plain. Here Europe's longest rivers flow. The Volga, which is 2,194 miles, is the longest of them all.

Natural Vegetation

Over the centuries farmers have changed the natural vegetation of Europe by cultivation. Mixed forests of conifers and broadleaved deciduous trees once covered much of the continent, but these were cut down to make way for farming. Large forests survive in parts of Scandinavia, where the summers are too short to grow crops. Land north of the Arctic Circle is covered with tundra. Across south-eastern Russia stretch treeless plains called steppes. Wide areas of the Mediterranean are covered with low woody bushes and heaths.

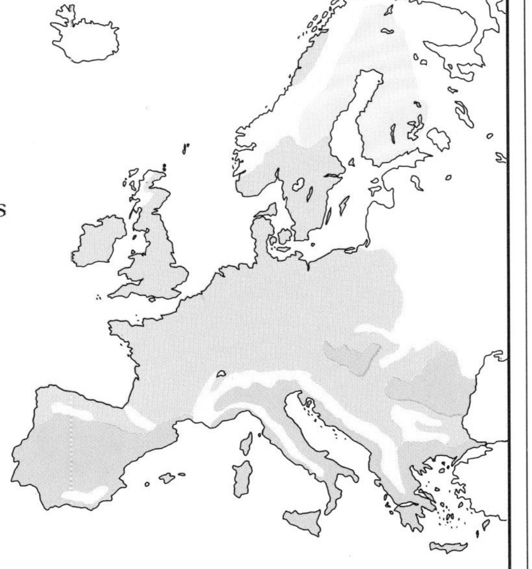

- Tundra/Mountain
- Northern Forest
- Mixed/Broadleaf Forest
- Scrub

Temperate Grasslands

Fertile meadows and woodland (see below) make up the North European Plain from England to Finland.

Climate

Almost all of Europe lies in the cool temperate zone. Only the most northerly part is within the Arctic Circle. Western Europe is wetter than the east because nearly all the rain is brought by winds blowing from the Atlantic, which also bring warm air in winter. Eastern Europe has more extreme temperatures, with hot summers and bitterly cold winters. The Mediterranean has hot summers almost without rain, and in the winter it is seldom cold, except in the mountains.

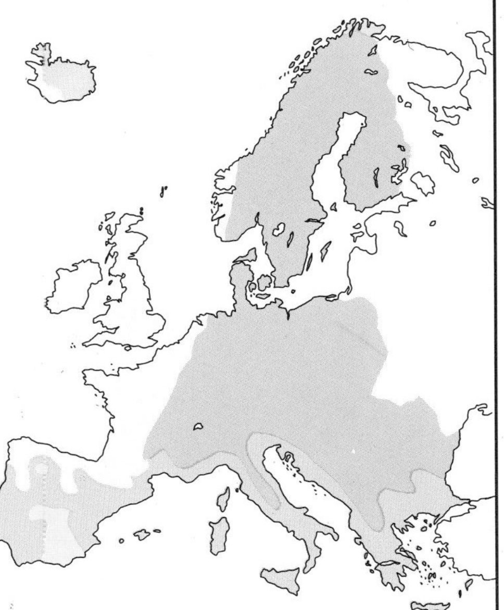

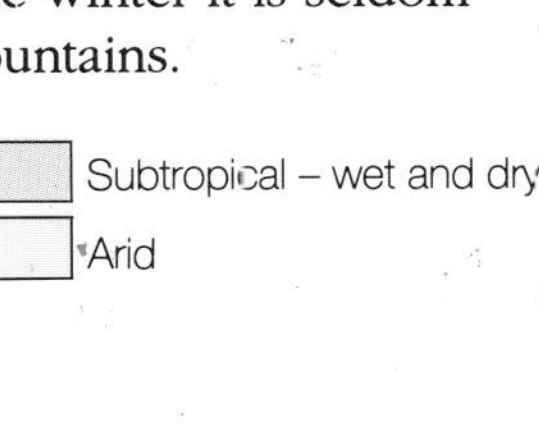

- Arctic/Subpolar
- Oceanic/Maritime
- Continental
- Subtropical – wet and dry
- Arid

Arctic Tundra

Only a few hardy plants, such as the Arctic mouse ear below, survive the harsh conditions of the tundra.

Europe's Varied Wildlife

Much of the wildlife is threatened.

SCANDINAVIA

Norway – Land of Conifers
In Norway, the coniferous forests of pine and spruce trees (see below) that cover a quarter of the land, are home to many birds (see above). Paper mills are situated at the mouths of rivers so that logs can be floated down to them and the products exported by sea.

The Scandinavian countries are Denmark, Sweden, Norway, Finland, and Iceland. Denmark is a small, flat, agricultural country with a dense population. Sweden and Finland consist largely of lakes and forests. Norway is a bare mountainous country with a long coastline. These last three have the lowest populations in Europe. Iceland is an island just south of the Arctic Circle.

Iceland – Land of Glaciers
Over a tenth of Iceland is covered by glaciers (see right). The largest is called Vatnajokull. At the same time, there is much volcanic activity.

FACT CHART

In 1963 a volcanic eruption in the sea created a new island, Surtsey, off the south coast of Iceland. Ten years later the nearby island of Heimaey had to be evacuated when a volcano erupted and destroyed a town.

Hammerfest in Norway is the world's northernmost town. From May to August the sun never sets, and from November to February it is dark all day.

Glittertind (8,103 feet) in Norway is the highest mountain.

Sweden's natural resources of water power, timber, and iron ore have made it one of the richest countries in the world.

Lake Vänern (2,155 square miles) in Sweden is the largest lake in Scandinavia.

Nearly a tenth of Finland consists of lakes. Raft-like ferries link the shores, but in winter the lakes freeze over and motorists drive over the ice.

Denmark consists of the Jutland Peninsula and over 400 islands.

Scale approximately 1:8,333,000
At the scale of this map the straight line distance from Helsinki (D4) to Göteborg (B4) is approximately 494 miles (795 km).

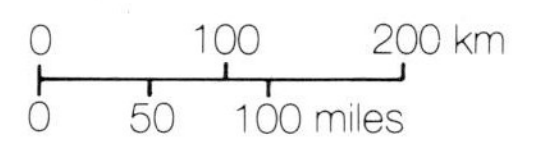

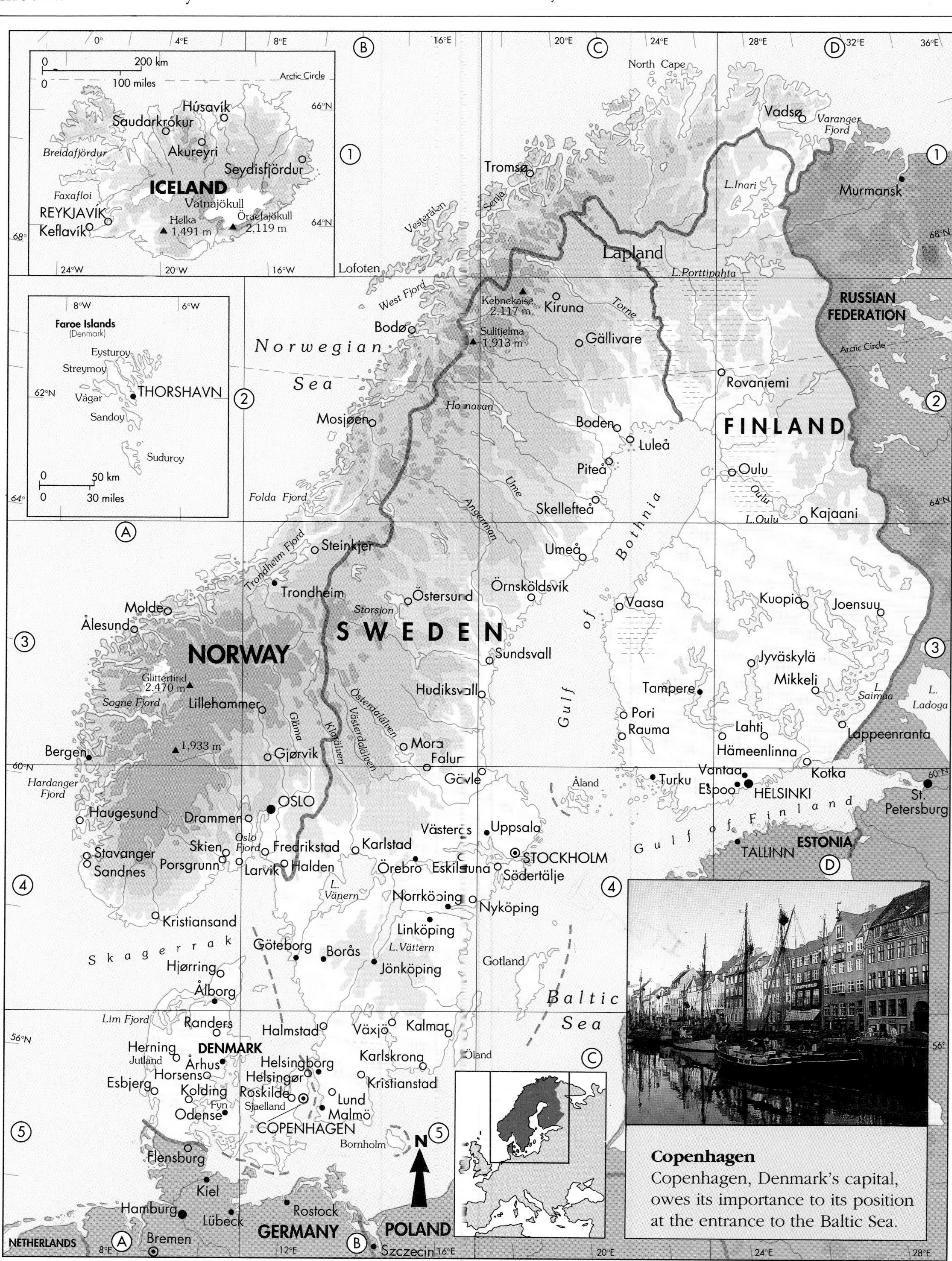

Copenhagen
Copenhagen, Denmark's capital, owes its importance to its position at the entrance to the Baltic Sea.

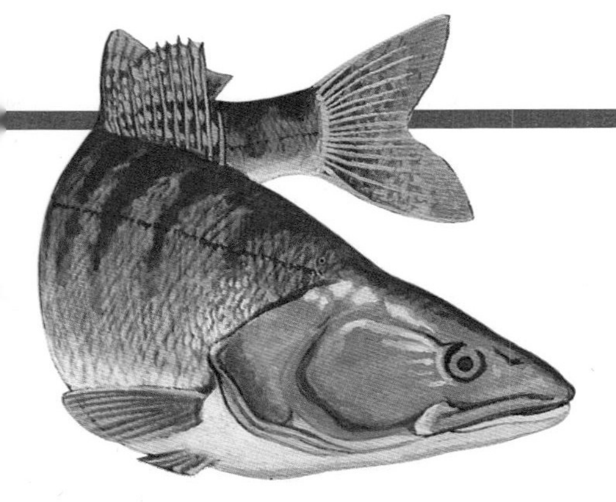

Land-locked Hungary
Hungary has no coastline, but the Tisza and Danube Rivers cross the Great Hungarian Plain and provide plenty of freshwater fish for food and sport.

Romania
The Black Sea (see right) has fine beaches and the summers are warm. It is a favorite holiday area.

Scale approximately 1:6,667,000
At the scale of this map the straight line distance from Gdansk (C1) to Bucharest (E4) is approximately 761 miles (1,226 km).

0 100 200 km
0 50 100 miles

Eastern Europe is an area of contrasts. Poland is part of the North European Plain. The land is mainly agricultural. Austria and Romania are mountainous; the Czech and Slovak Republics are a mixture of fertile plains and high mountains. Hungary has low hills in the north, but is dominated by the vast Great Hungarian Plain where herds of horses roam. The climate is cold in winter and warm in summer.

The Historic Cities of Poland
Many towns in Poland, such as Warsaw (see above), were ruined in World War 2. Many have now been restored to their former glory.

FACT CHART

- Austria is one of Europe's most mountainous countries. Ranges and spurs of the Alps cover about 70 percent of the country.
- On January 1st 1993 Czechoslovakia split into two. The Czech Republic is in the west and the Slovak Republic is in the east.
- Lake Balaton in northwest Hungary is a favorite holiday resort. It covers an area of 245 square miles.
- Poland is one of the world's largest producers of meat, and the third largest producer of coal.
- Ploesti is the center of the Romanian oil industry. Romania is self-sufficient in oil and exports its surplus.

Austria – a Center of Culture
Vienna, the capital city of Austria, is one of the great cultural centers of Europe.

CENTRAL EUROPE

Germany, the wealthiest country in Europe, extends across much of Central Europe. The north, a low, flat plain, rises in the south towards the Alps. Belgium and the Netherlands are both small, flat countries. Much of the Netherlands is below sea level. The Dutch have built huge dykes to keep out the sea and drained large areas for farming. Switzerland and Liechtenstein, by contrast, are mountainous.

The Netherlands
The Dutch port of Rotterdam is the largest in the world. With over 75 miles of quayside it is one of the busiest ports in Europe.

Swiss Alps
The Swiss Alps are popular with tourists for their flowers and skiing. Mountains cover 70 percent of the land.

The Center of the EC
The headquarters of the European Community are in Brussels. Belgium was one of the first six countries to found the EC in 1957.

FACT CHART

- In the last 800 years the Netherlands has lost about 14 million acres of land to the sea and reclaimed at least 17 million acres.
- The world's longest road tunnel, St. Gotthard (over 10 miles), runs under the Alps in Switzerland.
- In Belgium the Flemings, who speak Flemish, live in the north. The French-speaking Walloons live in the south.
- The River Rhine in Germany, over 620 miles long, carries more shipping than any other river in the world.
- Liechtenstein, one of the smallest countries in the world at 62 square miles, has a population of 25,000.

Scale approximately 1:5,000,000
At the scale of this map the straight line distance from Geneva (B5) to Rostock (C2) is approximately 605 miles (974 km).

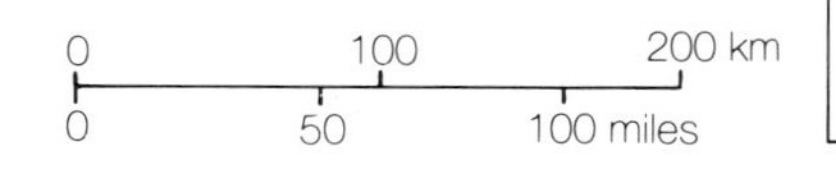

German Castles
The River Rhine is famous for its ancient castles (see above). It has been an important trading route for centuries.

BRITISH ISLES

The British Isles consist of Britain, Ireland and some small islands near their coasts. Britain contains England, Scotland, and Wales. Ireland is divided into Northern Ireland, which is part of the United Kingdom, and Ireland (Eire).

The landscape is very varied. Wales and Scotland have ranges of low mountains. But except for the Pennines, England is low-lying.

English Woodlands
Much of England was once covered by forests of trees such as the oak (see left). Most of these were felled for farm and building land.

The Emerald Isle
Ireland was once part of the United Kingdom, but in 1922 it became an independent republic. The six counties of Northern Ireland (Ulster) stayed with the United Kingdom. The shamrock (see above) is the national emblem of Ireland.

Welsh Castles
Wales was divided into several small independent kingdoms until Edward I conquered the Welsh in the 13th century. Edward built several castles which still survive (see above). The Welsh language is taught in the schools and spoken by many people.

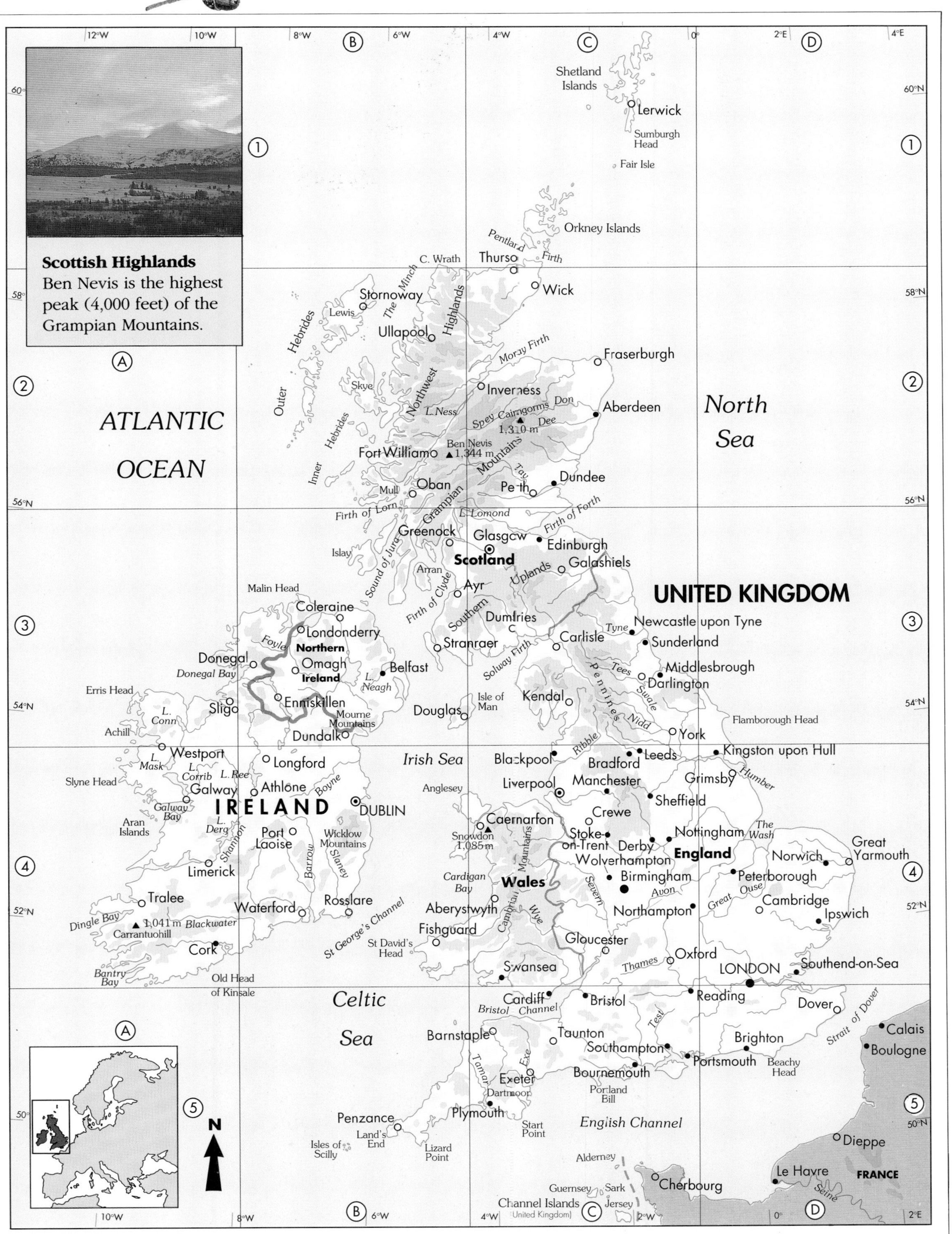

Scottish Highlands
Ben Nevis is the highest peak (4,000 feet) of the Grampian Mountains.

FACT CHART

- London is the largest city in Europe. It extends over an area of 630 square miles, and has about 8 million inhabitants.
- Nowhere in the United Kingdom is further than 70 miles from the sea.
- Scotland consists of a mainland and about 780 islands, many of which are uninhabited.
- The longest river in Ireland, the Shannon is 238 miles long.
- The highest point in Ireland is Carrantuohill (3,412 feet) in the southwest.
- The highest peak in Wales (3,600 feet) is in Snowdonia.

Scale approximately 1:5,250,000
At the scale of this map the straight line distance from Plymouth (C5) to Lerwick (C1) is approximately 684 miles (1,101 km).

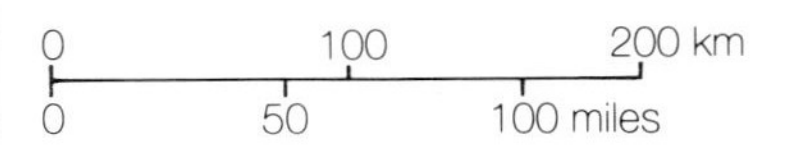

Wine and Cheese
Food is a major industry, over 250 French wines and 240 French cheeses are made (see above). The largest vineyard on earth (2,000,000 acres) is in southern France.

Scale approximately 1:5,555,000
At the scale of this map the straight line distance from Marseilles (D4) to Brest (A2) is approximately 592 miles (953 km).

0 100 200 km
0 50 100 miles

France, the second largest country in Europe, stretches almost 620 miles from north to south and from east to west. Almost a third of the land is cultivated and at least 25 percent of this is pasture. One-fifth of exports come from farm goods. Large supplies of coal, iron ore, bauxite (aluminum ore), sulfur, and natural gas have fueled a thriving industrial economy. With modern factories and the latest technology, France is among the top five industrial exporters.

Paris
The historic center of Paris is a major tourist attraction. Many people visit the famous Champs-Elysées and Arc de Triomphe (see right).

Luxembourg is a land of farms and forests with huge deposits of iron ore in the northeast. The small country of Monaco consists of two towns – Monaco and Monte Carlo.

FACT CHART

- France, the second largest country in Europe, has a highly developed transport system. Extensive highways, inland railways, and waterways enable rapid transport of people and goods across Europe.
- There are 22 regions in France, each with a Regional Council elected by the local people. Each region is divided into departments – there are 95 in all.
- France is a multiparty democracy. The French Parliament consists of two sets of elected members – the senate which has little legislative power (319 members) and the National Assembly, the principle law-making body (577 members). The elected President, who appoints the Prime Minister, resides at the Elysée Palace.
- Luxembourg, established in 963, is one of the oldest independent countries.
- Monaco is tiny – only 0.6 square miles.

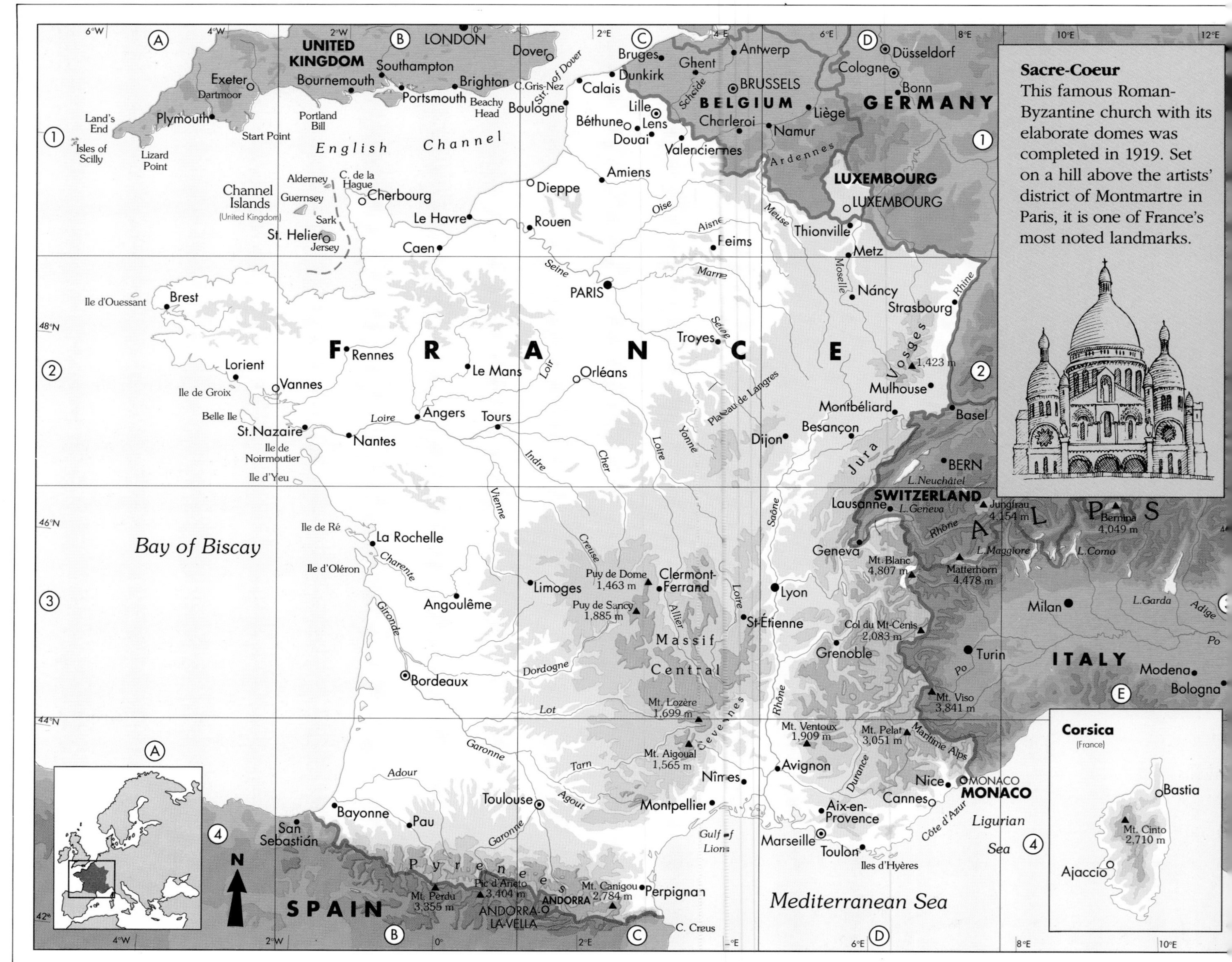

Sacre-Coeur
This famous Roman-Byzantine church with its elaborate domes was completed in 1919. Set on a hill above the artists' district of Montmartre in Paris, it is one of France's most noted landmarks.

SPAIN and PORTUGAL

FACT CHART

- Spain is the third largest country in Europe. Portugal lies on the west coast of Spain, bordering the Atlantic Ocean.
- Spain is a mountainous country, the chief mountain ranges being the Pyrenees, the Cordillera Cantábrica, and the Sierra de Gredos. Spain's highest mountain, at over 11,200 feet, is the volcano Teide on Tenerife, the Canary Islands. Portugal's highest point, located in the Serra da Estrela, is 6,000 feet above sea level.
- Spain is among the top ten industrial countries in the world.
- Both Spain and Portugal are members of the EC.

Madrid
Madrid, the capital of Spain since 1561, is the seat of government and an industrial and communications center (see right).

Spain and Portugal occupy the Iberian Peninsula in southwest Europe. Spain includes two groups of islands – the Canaries and the Balearics.

Spain's economy is mostly based on services, including tourism, industry, and agriculture.

Large quantities of tomatoes, oranges, and wine are exported. Copper, lead, and zinc are mined in the Sierra Morena mountains, and reserves of iron and coal help fuel industry.

About 40 percent of Portugal is arable land and another 40 percent is covered by forests and woods. There is a mixed economy based on light and heavy engineering, particularly ship building and repair, and agriculture – wine, figs, and cork are all exported.

Scale approximately 1:5,000,000
At the scale of this map the straight line distance from Lisbon (A3) to Barcelona (E2) is approximately 623 miles (1,009 km).

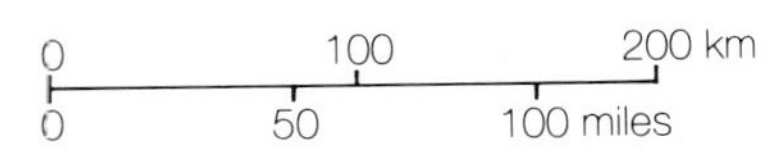

Holy Week
Spain is renowned for its festivals such as Holy Week – the week before Easter (see above).

Hilltop Castles
The medieval castles of Spain and Portugal (see below) reflect their historic past.

ITALY and THE BALKAN STATES

Southern Europe consists of three great peninsulas: the Iberian Peninsula (Spain and Portugal), Italy, and the Balkan Peninsula. The Balkans (the Turkish word for mountains) includes Albania, Bulgaria, mainland Greece, European Turkey, parts of Croatia, Slovenia, Bosnia and Hercegovina, and Yugoslavia.

Some of these countries are the poorest in Europe, depending mostly on farming, although the conditions are not favorable. The climate is hot and dry, and the land mountainous. Fruit is a main crop and wheat and barley grow during the winter and ripen in early summer. Many people make a living from fishing. Yugoslavia has many resources including coal, lead, zinc, and copper.

Good beaches and plenty of sunshine have made many areas popular with tourists.

Yugoslavia
Belgrade (see above), the capital of Yugoslavia, is situated at the gateway from the Balkans to Central Europe. In April 1992, three former Yugoslavian states became independent countries – Croatia, Slovenia, and Bosnia and Hercegovina.

Bulgaria
Sofia (see above) is Bulgaria's capital city, and is known for its educational and cultural facilities. It was badly damaged in World War 2 and much of it has been rebuilt.

Wildlife
In some of the wilder areas of the region, wild boar (see above), wolves, wild goats, and ibex can be found.

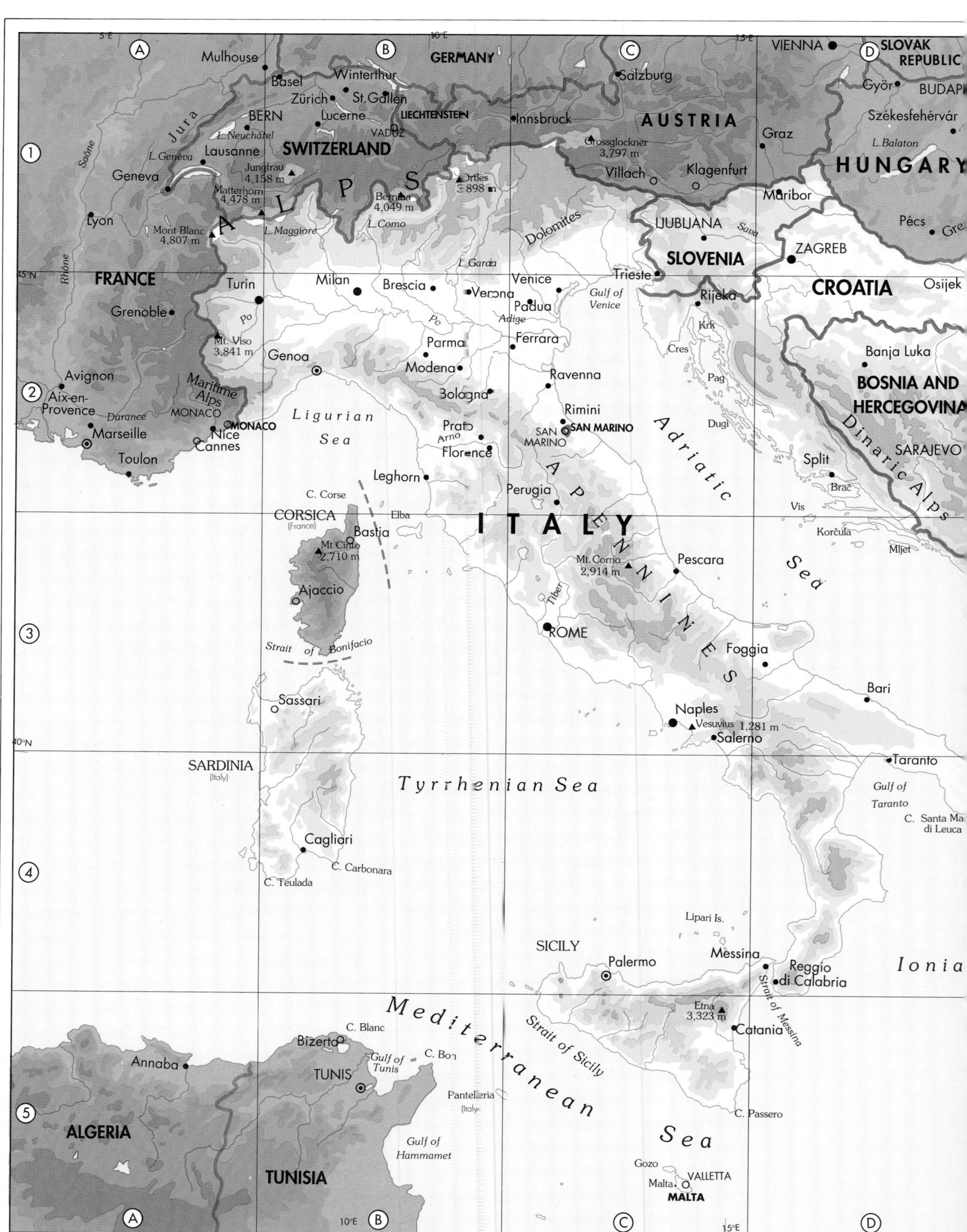

Italian Wheatfields
The Italians eat much bread and pasta. Wheat is an important crop on the northern plains, and in Apulia and Sicily.

Lands of Vines
Grapes are grown all over Italy and Greece. Each region produces its own type of wine.

Mediterranean Fruits
Greece is a leading exporter of lemons. The climate is ideal for growing citrus fruits. Southern Italy and Sicily grow lemons, oranges, peaches, grapefruit, and olives.

The Pantheon
The Pantheon (see below) is one of the sights of Rome. Many Ancient Roman buildings still survive in Italy.

FACT CHART

- Vesuvius, above the Bay of Naples, is the only active volcano on the European mainland.
- Greece has 166 inhabited islands. The largest of these is Crete. There are also 1,259 uninhabited ones.
- Slovenia's highest peak, Triglav, is 9,396 feet.
- Bulgaria is famous for its red roses, which grow in the valley of Kazanlyk, sheltered by the slopes of the Balkans.
- Albania is known locally as Shqiperi, which means "eagles' country" – an apt name for such a remote, mountainous land.
- Italy's longest river is the Po (418 miles); its largest lake is Lake Garda (143 square miles).

Scale approximately 1:5,882,000
At the scale of this map the straight line distance from Athens (F4) to Turin (A2) is approximately 963 miles (1,550 km).

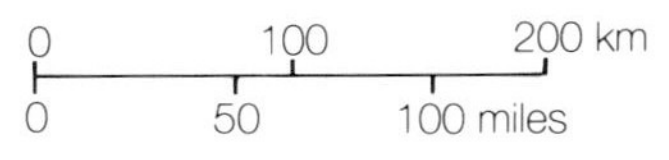

AFRICA

Rain Forests
Over 50 percent of Africa's natural rain forests (see below) have been cleared for timber and farming. Tree crops like cocoa, oil palm, and rubber grow well. Oil from the African oil palm (see above) is used to make margarine and soap.

Desert Sands
There are two main desert regions in Africa – the Sahara in the north and the Kalahari and Namib in the south. The plants that grow there, called succulents, store water in their roots, stems, or leaves (see below).

Africa, the warmest and second largest continent, extends almost 2,500 miles north and south of the Equator. It is a land of contrasts. Tropical rain forests grow around the Equator. These give way to huge plains of tropical grasslands that support herds of animals, especially in the wet season. Desert regions in the north and south have such low rainfall that few plants and animals can survive.

A few mountain ranges break up this vast plateau. The highest peaks, such as Mount Kenya and Kilimanjaro (Uhuru), are always covered in snow.

Population
Health care has improved greatly, especially for children, and this has led to a rapid increase in the total population. However, some areas cannot support large populations – of a total population of 670 million, almost 550 million live south of the Sahara. In the deserts, only fertile oases can support small settlements of people.

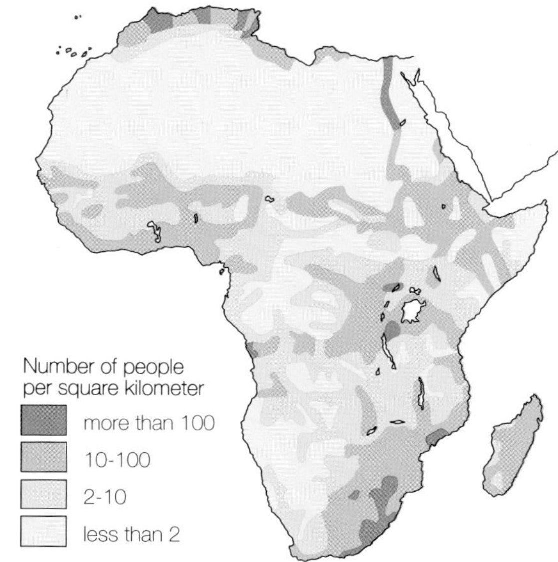
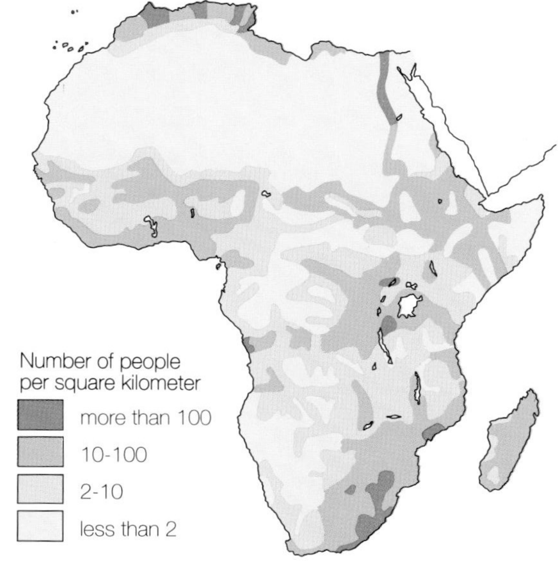

Madeira (Portugal)
Casablanca
RABAT
Fez
Oran
ALGIERS
Constantine
MOROCCO
TUNISIA
Canary Islands (Spain)
EL AAIÚN
Tropic of Cancer
WESTERN SAHARA (claimed by Morocco)
ALGERIA
MAURITANIA
NOUAKCHOTT
Senegal
MALI
NIGER
DAKAR
SENEGAL
THE GAMBIA
BANJUL
BAMAKO
BISSAU
GUINEA BISSAU
BURKINA FASO
NIAMEY
Zinder
GUINEA
Bobo-Dioulasso
OUAGADOUGOU
CONAKRY
BENIN
NIGERIA
FREETOWN
SIERRA LEONE
IVORY COAST
GHANA
TOGO
ABUJA
Ogbomosho
Benue
Niger
Bouaké
MONROVIA
LIBERIA
YAMOUSSOUKRO
Kumasi
PORTO NOVO
Ibadan
Lagos
Abidjan
ACCRA
LOMÉ
CAPE VERDE
PRAIA
Gulf of Guinea
MALABO
Douala
YAOUNDÉ
CAMEROON
EQUAT. GUINEA
SÃO TOMÉ AND PRÍNCIPE
SÃO TOMÉ
Equator
LIBREVILLE
Port Gentil
GABON
Pointe-Noire
Cabinda (Angola)
LUANDA
Lubango
ATLANTIC OCEAN
Tropic of Capricorn
30°N
20°N
10°N
15°N
0°
10°S
20°S
30°S
20°W
10°W
10°E

Natural Vegetation
The natural vegetation and landscape of Africa are very diverse – from the hot Sahara desert to lush tropical jungle and from snow-topped mountain peaks to hot grassy plains. Much of the rain forest has been cut down, but some forests, such as the Korup National Park, are now protected areas.

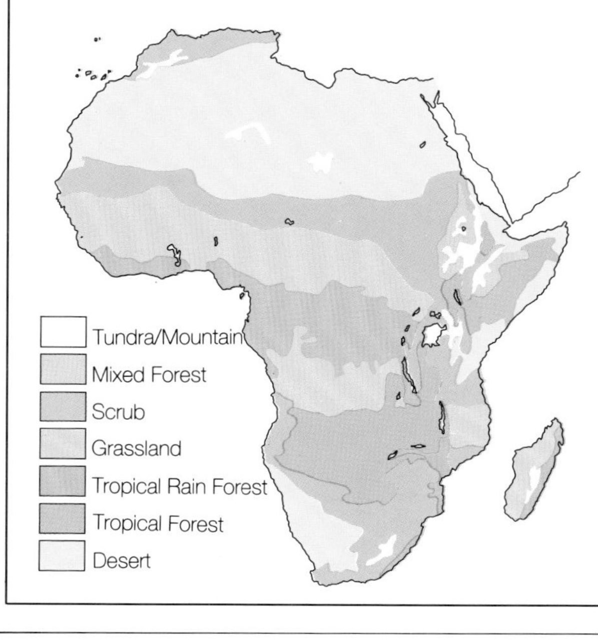

Climate
Africa's climate is generally warm and hot because it lies between the tropics. The amount of rainfall varies greatly throughout the continent, and this determines the type of vegetation and climate. Some areas suffer from periods of drought, which has led to thousands of people dying from starvation.

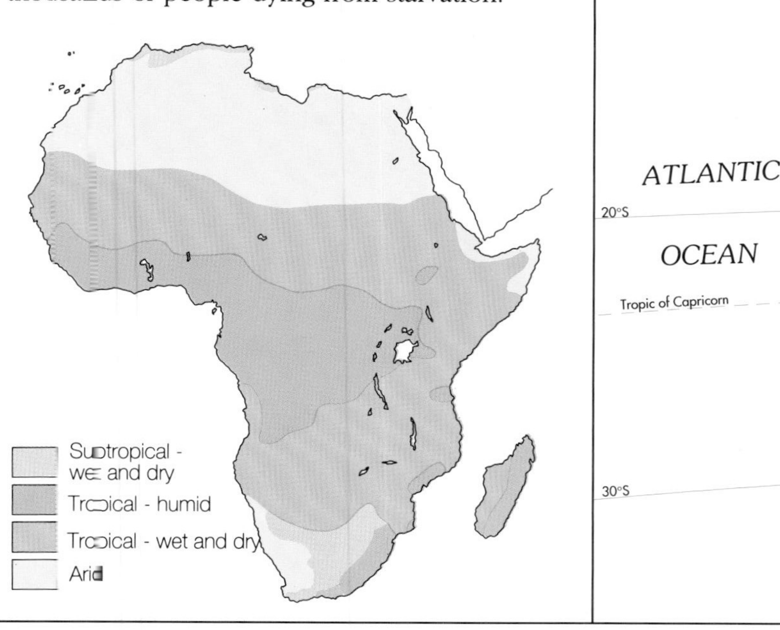

The Grasslands

The tropical grasslands, or savanna (see left), of Africa are home to lions, gazelles, zebras, and many other animals. Many of the plants, like the thorn trees, have long spines but this does not stop giraffes feeding on them (see right).

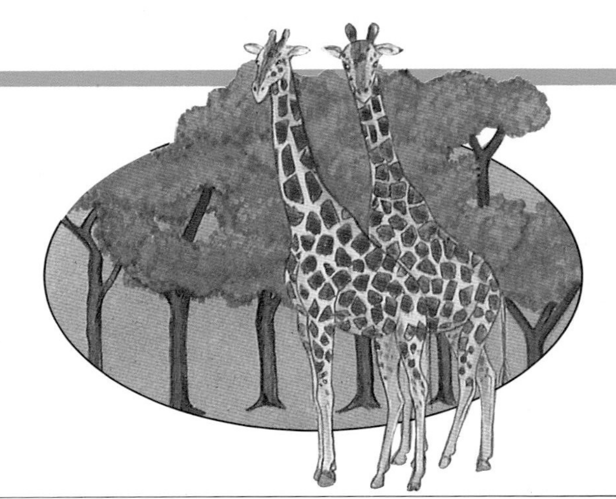

Health Care

Although medical advances have saved millions of lives, many children in Africa still die from childhood infections. Vaccination programs and effective health care are being introduced into many regions, such as here in Ethiopia (see below).

Food and Drink

Some vegetables, such as yams, are important staple foods in Africa. However, one local produce, coffee (see right), has spread throughout the world. It is now a widely cultivated plant prized for its seeds, which when dried and roasted make the commercial coffee bean.

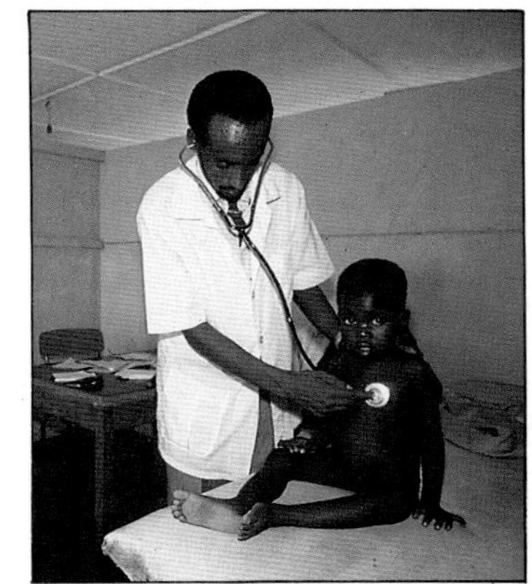

FACT CHART

- There are 52 independent countries in Africa, more than on any other continent. But most of them have fewer people than large cities such as London and Tokyo.
- Centuries ago, before Europeans colonized Africa, great empires flourished there. Some of their names, such as Benin and Zimbabwe, have been given to new, independent countries.

- Africa has vast deposits of copper, diamonds, gold, and oil. Some of the oldest known mines, in Swaziland, were mined for iron 43,000 years ago.
- The largest desert in the world, the Sahara, also has the highest sand dunes in the world – over 1,300 feet high and up to 3 miles long! However, only 30 percent of the Sahara is sand, the rest is rocky wasteland. It is also the sunniest place, with an average of 4,300 hours of sunshine a year.
- The longest river in the world, the Nile (4,135 miles) flows through North Africa to the Mediterranean Sea.

Scale approximately 1:32,000,000

0 500 1,000 km

0 300 600 miles

NORTH and WEST AFRICA

A land of contrasts, North Africa ranges from the warm plains of Morocco, where olives, vineyards, and citrus groves flourish, to the Atlas Mountains and the biggest desert in the world – the Sahara. The central plains are mostly grasslands, where the people farm their own plots of land and grow cash crops such as groundnuts.

Tropical forests border West Africa from the Gulf of Guinea inland. Many of these countries are watered by the mighty Niger. Wealthier than their neighbors, these lands are rich in tin, oil, bauxite, and diamonds.

Rain Forests
The lands close to the Equator are covered with dense rain forests. In West Africa they spread inland from the Gulf of Guinea. The hot, wet climate encourages growth of dense vegetation, which supports a huge variety of wildlife, like the bushbaby above.

Fruits of the Forests
The plant below, katemfe, is a natural sweetener. It is found in the tropical rain forests of West Africa. Used commercially, one-tenth of an ounce of katemfe extract makes 5 tons of sweetener.

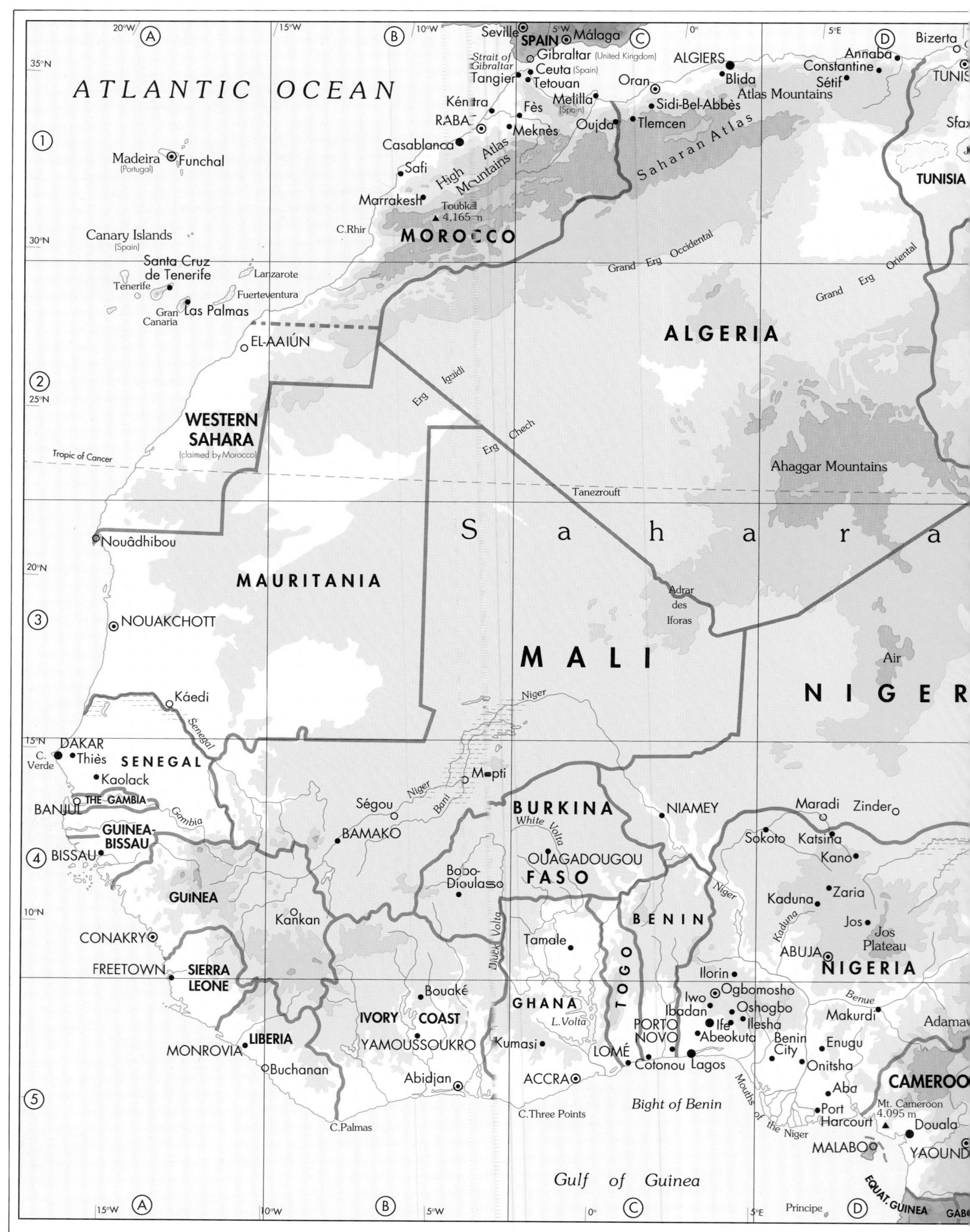

Atlas Mountains
The Atlas Mountains (left) cross Morocco and extend across north Algeria into Tunisia. They are divided into three main regions. The Rif Atlas bordering the Mediterranean rises 8,000 feet above sea level. To the south is the Middle Atlas. Farther south still, the High Atlas contains Morocco's highest peak, Jebel Toubkal, at 13,665 feet.

Village Life
Many villages in Nigeria and Chad (see above) do not have running water. The people often wash their clothes and cooking pots in the river and lakes.

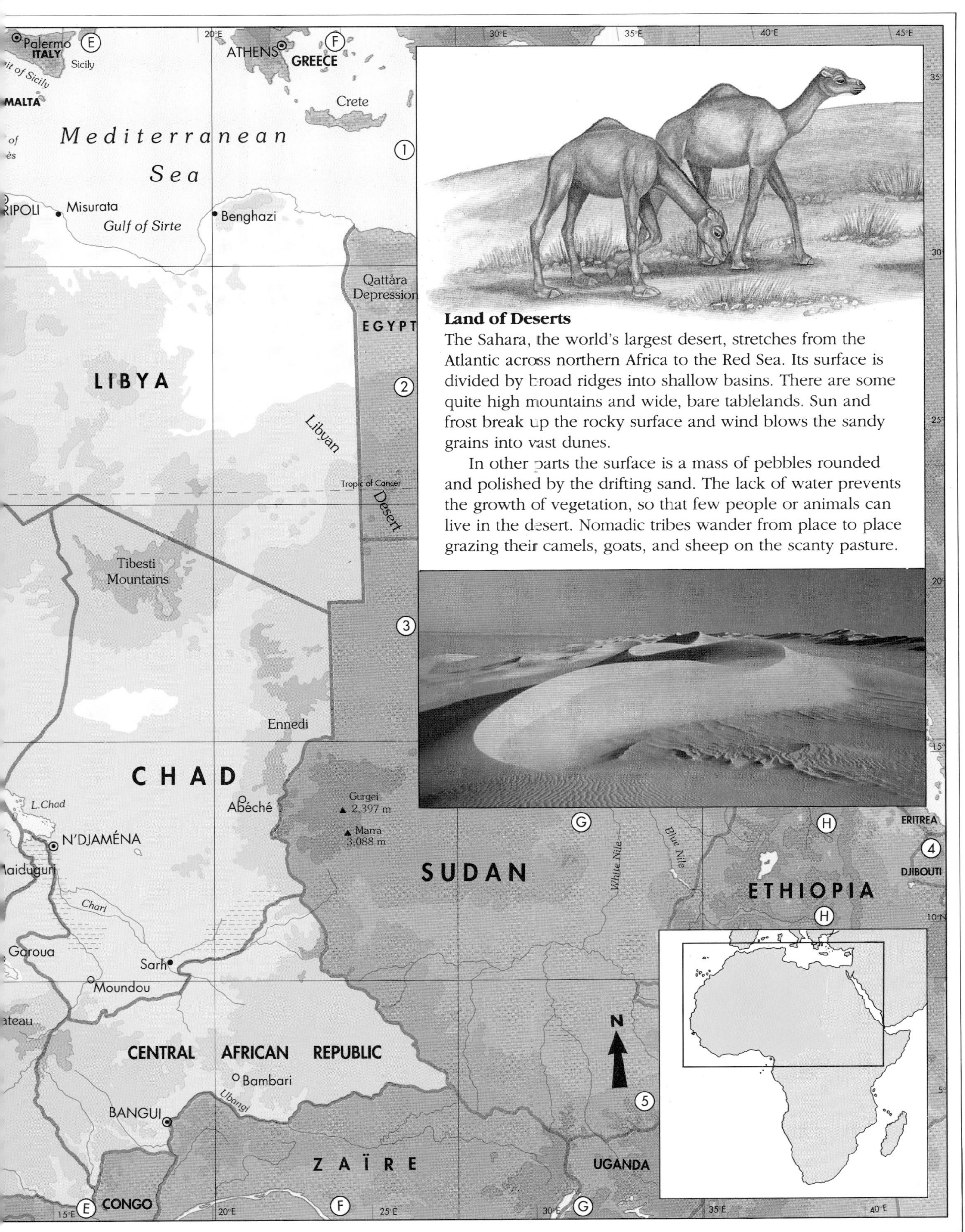

Land of Deserts
The Sahara, the world's largest desert, stretches from the Atlantic across northern Africa to the Red Sea. Its surface is divided by broad ridges into shallow basins. There are some quite high mountains and wide, bare tablelands. Sun and frost break up the rocky surface and wind blows the sandy grains into vast dunes.

In other parts the surface is a mass of pebbles rounded and polished by the drifting sand. The lack of water prevents the growth of vegetation, so that few people or animals can live in the desert. Nomadic tribes wander from place to place grazing their camels, goats, and sheep on the scanty pasture.

FACT CHART

- The River Niger flows for nearly 2,600 miles from its source in the southern highlands of Guinea into the Atlantic Ocean.
- Lake Chad is the remnant of an inland sea on the southern edge of the Sahara Desert. Four countries – Chad, Cameroon, Niger, and Nigeria – share the water, which is seldom more than 23 feet deep.
- In Ghana a great dam built across the River Volta has created a lake 250 miles long. The water is used to irrigate dry land and provide hydroelectric power.
- Libya has the largest oil reserves in Africa – the tenth largest in the world.

- Cave paintings of animals, including domestic cattle, suggest that the Sahara Desert was once wet enough to support plants and animals. Now the desert is expanding even further into Chad, Mali, and Senegal.

Scale approximately 1:15,957,000
At the scale of this map the straight line distance from Algiers (C1) to N'djamena (E4) is approximately 1,977 miles (3,183 km).

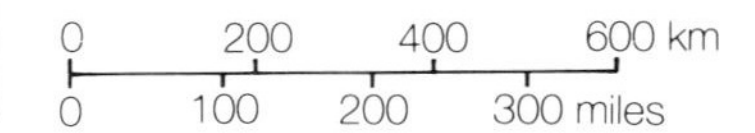

NILE VALLEY and EAST AFRICA

The Great Rift Valley – the largest crack in the Earth's crust – provides the most spectacular scenery in East Africa. In Kenya, the valley walls reach a height of 4,000 feet. The Eastern Rift ends at Lake Nyasa (Malawi); the Western Rift at Lake Tanganyika (4,710 feet deep).

The Nile delta is the most densely populated area. The wide plain is crossed by many channels and covered with fertile silt. Rice, cotton, and vegetables are grown. But beyond the range of the Nile floodwater, Egypt and Sudan are mostly desert.

The Masai People
The Masai travel in Kenya and Tanzania with their herds. The men become junior then senior warriors (see below).

Ancient Egypt
From early times people have lived in the fertile valley of the Nile. The golden mask of Tutankhamun (see above) from Luxor, and the pyramids and Sphinx (see below) near Cairo, are signs of one of the world's earliest civilizations.

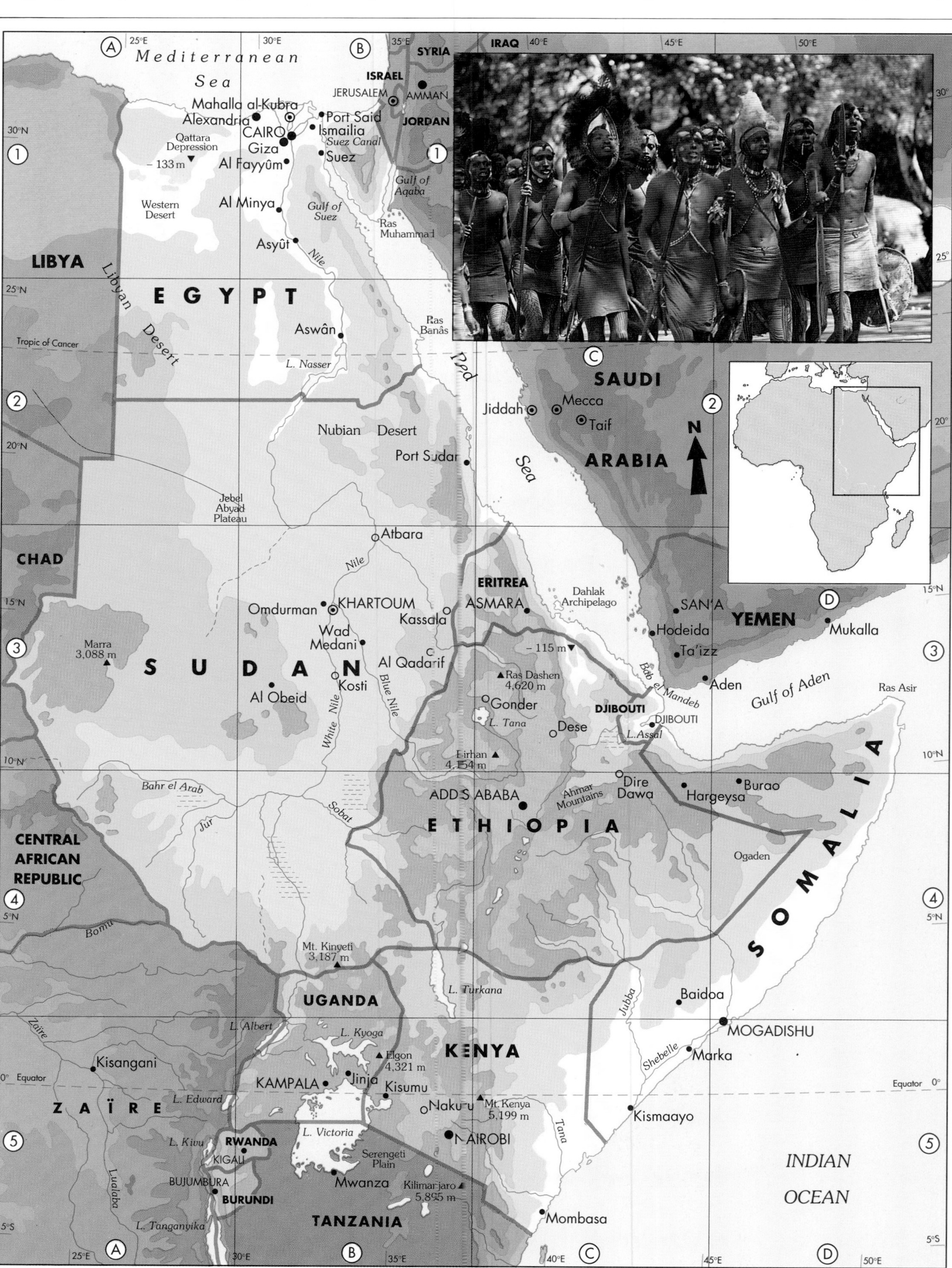

FACT CHART

● Lake Assal in Djibouti is the lowest point in Africa at over 450 feet below sea level.

● The Aswan High Dam on the Nile is 2 miles long and 360 feet high. It has created a huge artificial lake, Lake Nasser, and greatly increased the area of irrigated land.

● Lake Victoria, Africa's largest lake and the second largest in the world, is 255 miles from north to south, and 155 miles broad. It stands at an altitude of 3,700 feet.

● The Red Sea, one of the saltiest in the world, separates Africa and Asia. It is long and narrow – about 1,200 miles from end-to-end and 125–250 miles broad.

Scale approximately 1:17,273,000
At the scale of this map the straight line distance from Cairo (B1) to Mombasa (C5) is approximately 2,409 miles (3,879 km).

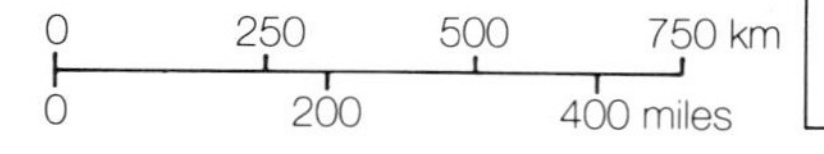

CENTRAL and SOUTHERN AFRICA

Animals of the African Plains
The grasslands of central Africa are home to many animals including antelopes, giraffes, zebras, and lions.

Central Africa has a tropical climate and much of it is covered in savanna grasslands. Many of the people depend on agriculture for their livelihood, but mining is also important.

South of the Zambezi the trees and tall grass give way to the dry, shrubby plains of the Kalahari Desert. In contrast, the open grassland, or veld, of South Africa is good farmland, rich in minerals.

Mining
Diamond mining is an important source of income in several African countries.

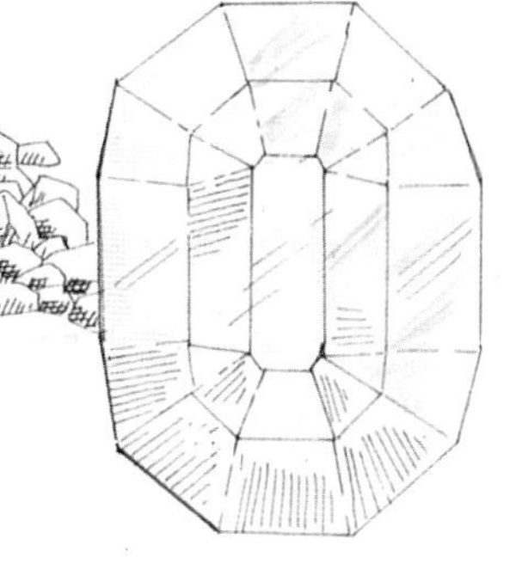

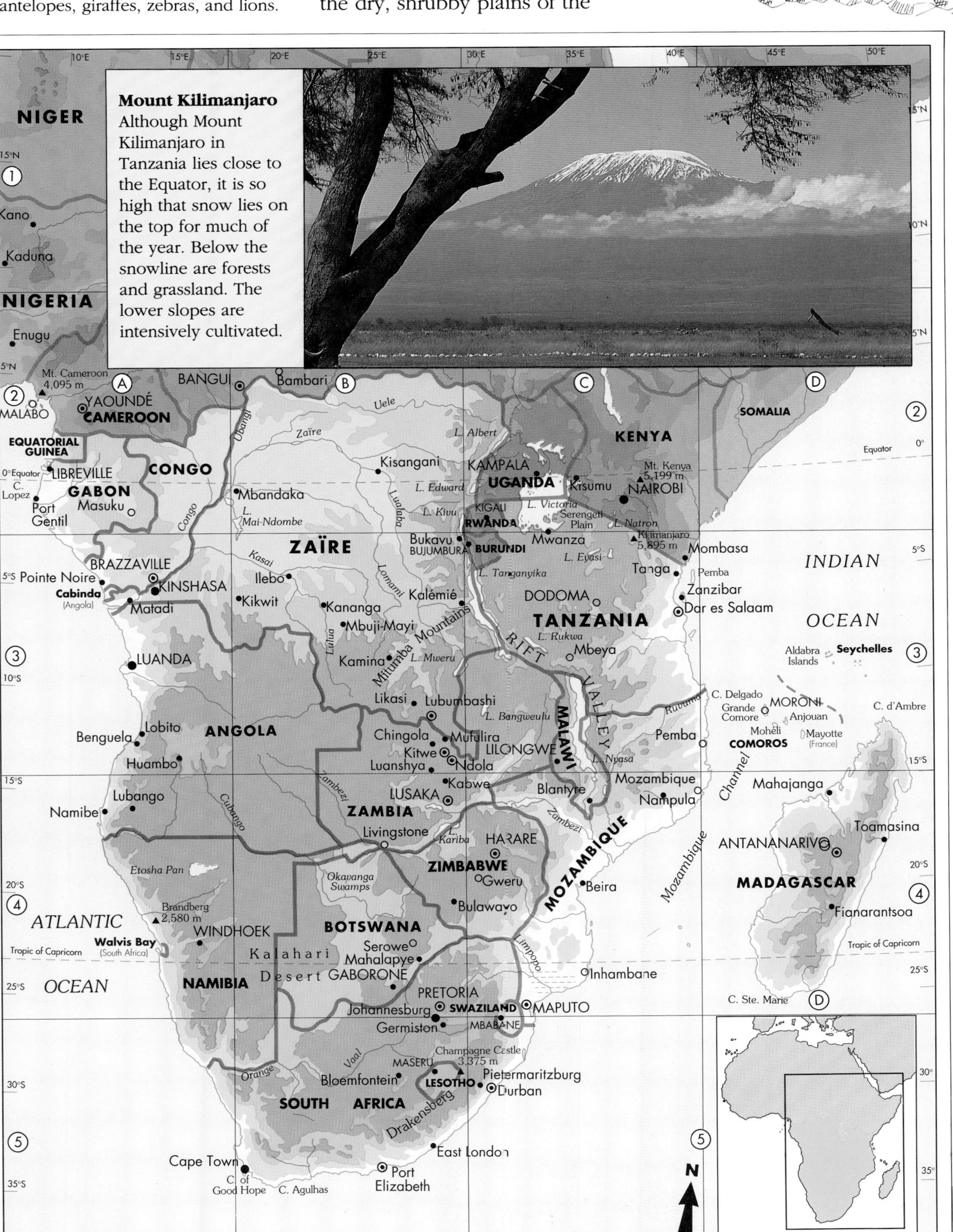

Mount Kilimanjaro
Although Mount Kilimanjaro in Tanzania lies close to the Equator, it is so high that snow lies on the top for much of the year. Below the snowline are forests and grassland. The lower slopes are intensively cultivated.

Victoria Falls
The Victoria Falls on the River Zambezi are over 1 mile wide and drop for 355 feet. The roar of water can be heard for 25 miles.

FACT CHART

- Mount Kilimanjaro is Africa's highest mountain. Kawenzi Peak (16,896 feet) and Kibo Peak (19,340 feet) are snow-capped and joined by a col, or pass.
- Madagascar, a large island off the southeast coast of Africa, has many unique animal and plant species not found in the rest of Africa.
- The Congo is the second longest river in Africa, flowing 2,900 miles from Zambia to the Atlantic Ocean.
- South Africa, the wealthiest African country, has large reserves of natural resources, including diamonds, gold, iron, uranium, and coal.

Scale approximately 1:25,330,000
At the scale of this map the straight line distance from Malabo (A2) to Dar es Salaam (C3) is approximately 2,278 miles (3,700 km).

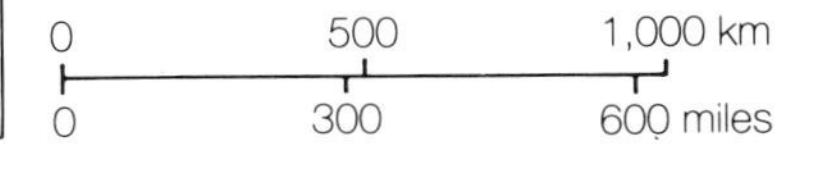

Natural Resources
Northern parts of Asia are very rich in mineral resources. Gold, silver, diamonds, and other gemstones are all found in Siberia (see above).

Desert
Asia has both hot and cold deserts. The Thar Desert (see above) is swept by hot, dry winds that create vast sand dunes under the burning sun. The Gobi Desert of Mongolia and China is hot in summer, but the winters are long and bitterly cold.

Main Crops
Tea is a principal crop of India and southeast Asia. The tea bushes, grown in large plantations, are picked by hand, usually by women.

Asia is the world's largest continent – it occupies over one-third of the land surface. Stretching from the Arctic to the Equator and from the Urals to the Pacific Ocean, it is a land of great contrasts.

The climate ranges from some of the driest to the wettest, and the hottest to the coldest places in the world. The tundra of the extreme north gives way to the vast, unpeopled expanse of Siberia. Much of Asia is high – the central mountain ranges are the highest in the world. Their melting snows drain into the Indus, Ganges, Mekong, and Yangtze Rivers, providing water for the vast populations of India, China, and southeast Asia.

The Japanese islands, with the Philippines and Indonesia, ring the eastern part of Asia. This area is renowned for its many volcanoes and frequent earthquakes.

Scale approximately 1:40,000,000

0 500 1,000 1,500 km
0 300 600 900 miles

Farms and Farming
In many parts of Asia the people still use primitive farming methods. Oxen have been used for plowing for thousands of years (see left).

Family Life
Asians regard the family as very important. Grandparents, parent, aunts, uncles, and children often live together in an extended family (see below).

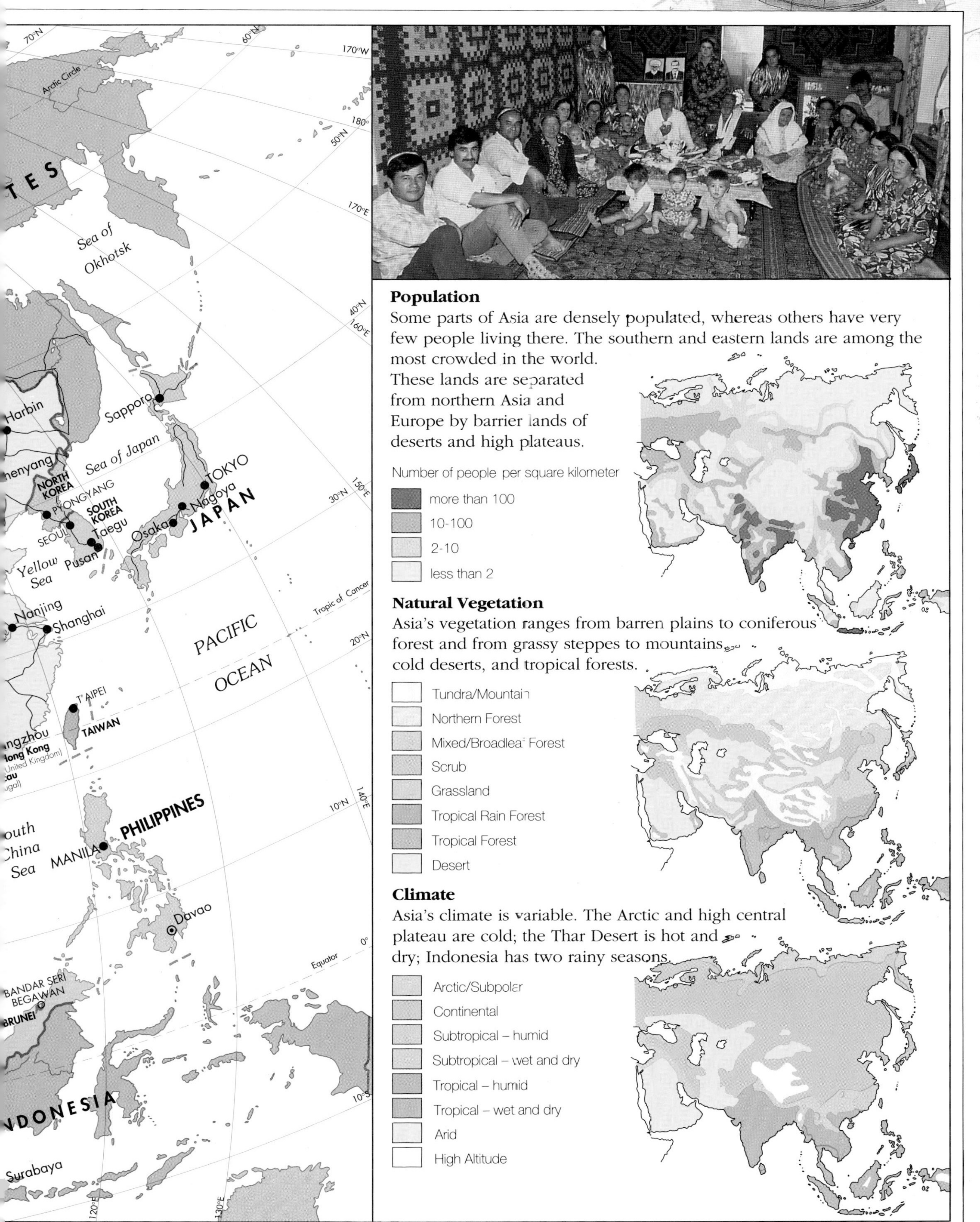

Population
Some parts of Asia are densely populated, whereas others have very few people living there. The southern and eastern lands are among the most crowded in the world. These lands are separated from northern Asia and Europe by barrier lands of deserts and high plateaus.

Natural Vegetation
Asia's vegetation ranges from barren plains to coniferous forest and from grassy steppes to mountains, cold deserts, and tropical forests.

Climate
Asia's climate is variable. The Arctic and high central plateau are cold; the Thar Desert is hot and dry; Indonesia has two rainy seasons.

A Diet of Rice
Rice is the staple diet of half the world's population. It is an important crop in the hot parts of Asia where there is enough rain. The rice plants are grown in paddy fields standing in water. If the crop fails, there is often famine.

FACT CHART

- Both the highest and lowest points on Earth are in Asia. Mount Everest is 29,028 feet at the highest peak. The shores of the Dead Sea are 1,309 feet below sea level.
- The largest lake in Asia is the Caspian Sea (about 143,000 square miles).
- The longest rivers in Asia are the Yangtze (3,500 miles), the Yenisey (3,400 miles), and the Huang He (3,395 miles).
- The Trans-Siberian Railway, which links Moscow with Vladivostok on the Pacific Ocean, is the longest railway line in the world. It is 5,800 miles long and the journey takes 7 days.
- Asia is the birthplace of all the major religions. Buddhism, Christianity, Confucianism, Islam, Hinduism, Judaism, Shinto, and Taoism all began in Asia.
- The main deserts of the region are the Gobi (500,000 square miles) and the Thar (74,000 square miles).
- The world's largest flower – Rafflesia – up to 3 feet across grows in the forests of Malaysia.

NORTHWEST ASIA

In December 1991 the Union of Soviet Socialist Republics (USSR) ceased to exist and the Commonwealth of Independent States (CIS) was founded by eleven former Soviet Republics. The three Baltic states of Estonia, Latvia, and Lithuania, and the former republic of Georgia have not joined the Commonwealth. It is an economic and political association of independent sovereign states.

Bounded by the Urals, northwest Asia is a land of forest and seas The region is important for agriculture, timber, and oil as well as tourism.

National Dress
Distinctive traditional costumes, like these from Georgia, are worn on special occasions in many regions.

The Ukraine Steppes
The "black soil" lands of the Ukrainian steppes are one of the most important wheat-producing areas of the world.

Estonia
Tallinn (see above), the capital of Estonia, is famous for its song festivals featuring thousands of singers.

FACT CHART

- The Caspian Sea (139,230 sq. miles) is the world's largest inland body of water. It was once joined to both the Black Sea and the Aral Sea.
- The River Volga, popularly known as "Mother Volga", is 2,300 miles long.
- The Aral Sea – the fourth largest inland sea – is strewn with 1,300 tiny islands.

Baltic Wildlife
The mixed woodlands of the region are home to a variety of animals including lynx, badgers (see right), deer, and elk.

Scale approximately 1:18,000,000
At the scale of this map the straight line distance from Riga (A3) to Baku (C5) is approximately 1,623 miles (2,614 km).

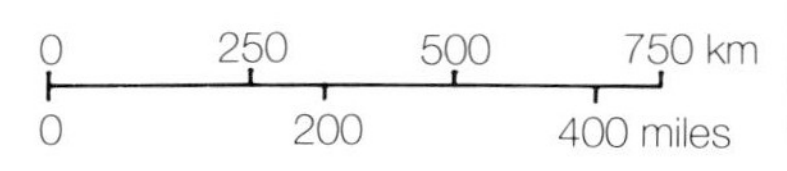

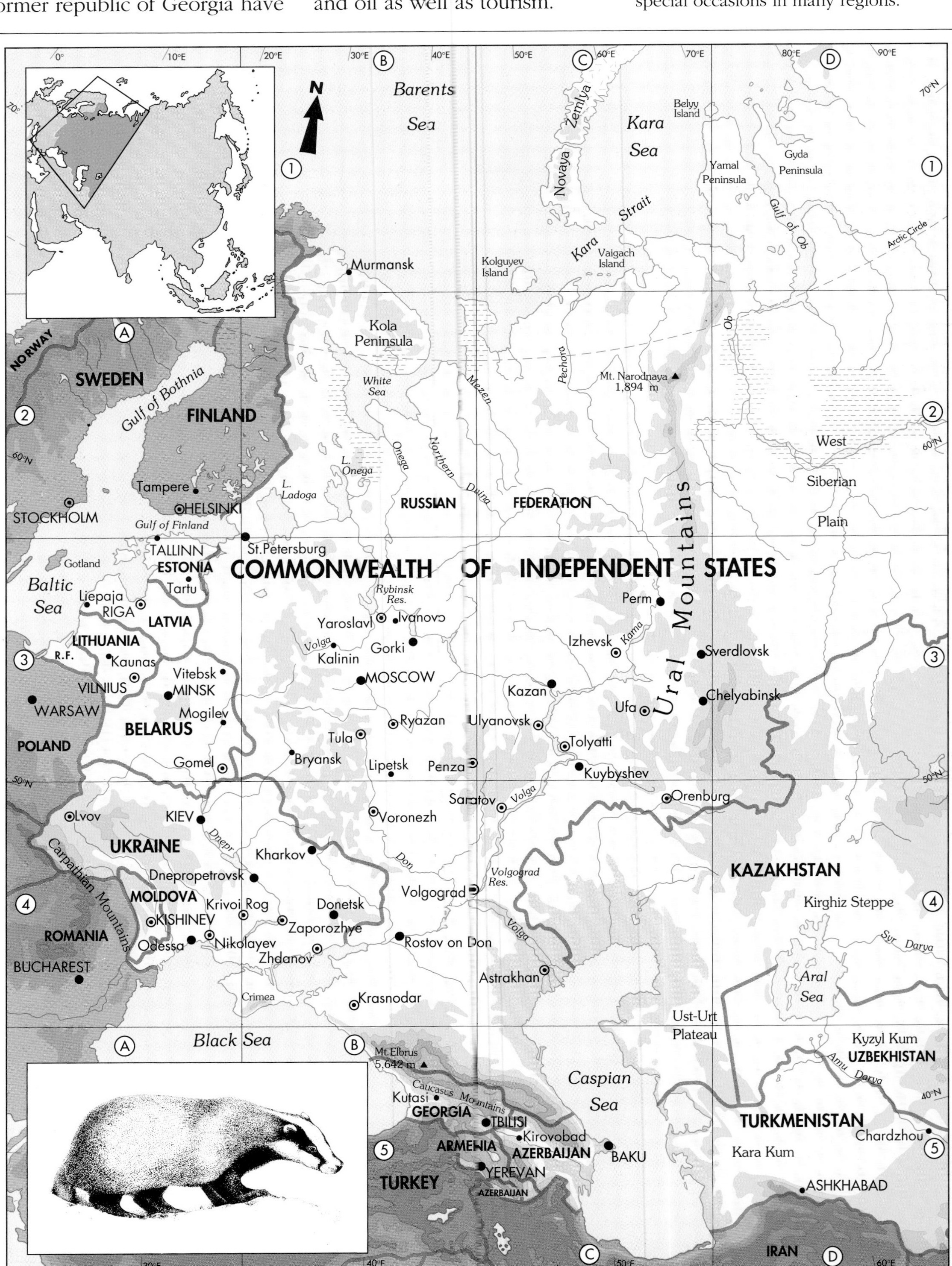

NORTH and CENTRAL ASIA

St Basil's Cathedral, Moscow
St Basil's Cathedral in Moscow's Red Square (see above) is a reminder of the Byzantine culture and architecture of earlier times.

Siberia (Tatar for "sleeping land") covers most of North and Central Asia. The vast western Siberian plain, drained by the Ob and Yenisey rivers, is low-lying and swampy with coniferous forests. The central plateau rises to 5,580 feet in the Putoran Mountains and is drained by the Lena River. Eastern Siberia is mountainous, with areas of steppe and tundra. Siberia is notorious for its long, cold winters with temperatures as low as –89°F.

Famous Food
Caviar, a valuable export and one of the world's most expensive foods, is produced mostly in the Caspian.

Siberian Plain
Siberia is rich in minerals, and there are many mining settlements. In winter (see above) the land is snow-covered.

FACT CHART

- Lake Baikal, 395 miles long, is the largest freshwater lake in Eurasia. At 5,700 feet deep it is the deepest lake in the world. It remains frozen for 4 months of the year.
- Over 350 rivers flow into Lake Baikal, but only one – the Angara – flows out.
- Verkoyansk and Omyyakon in northeast Siberia are the coldest inhabited places in the world with winter temperatures as low as –89°F.

Scale approximately 1:31,035,000
At the scale of this map the straight line distance from Omsk (B3) to Vladivostock (E3) is approximately 2,683 miles (4,320 km).

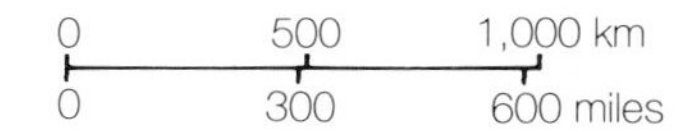

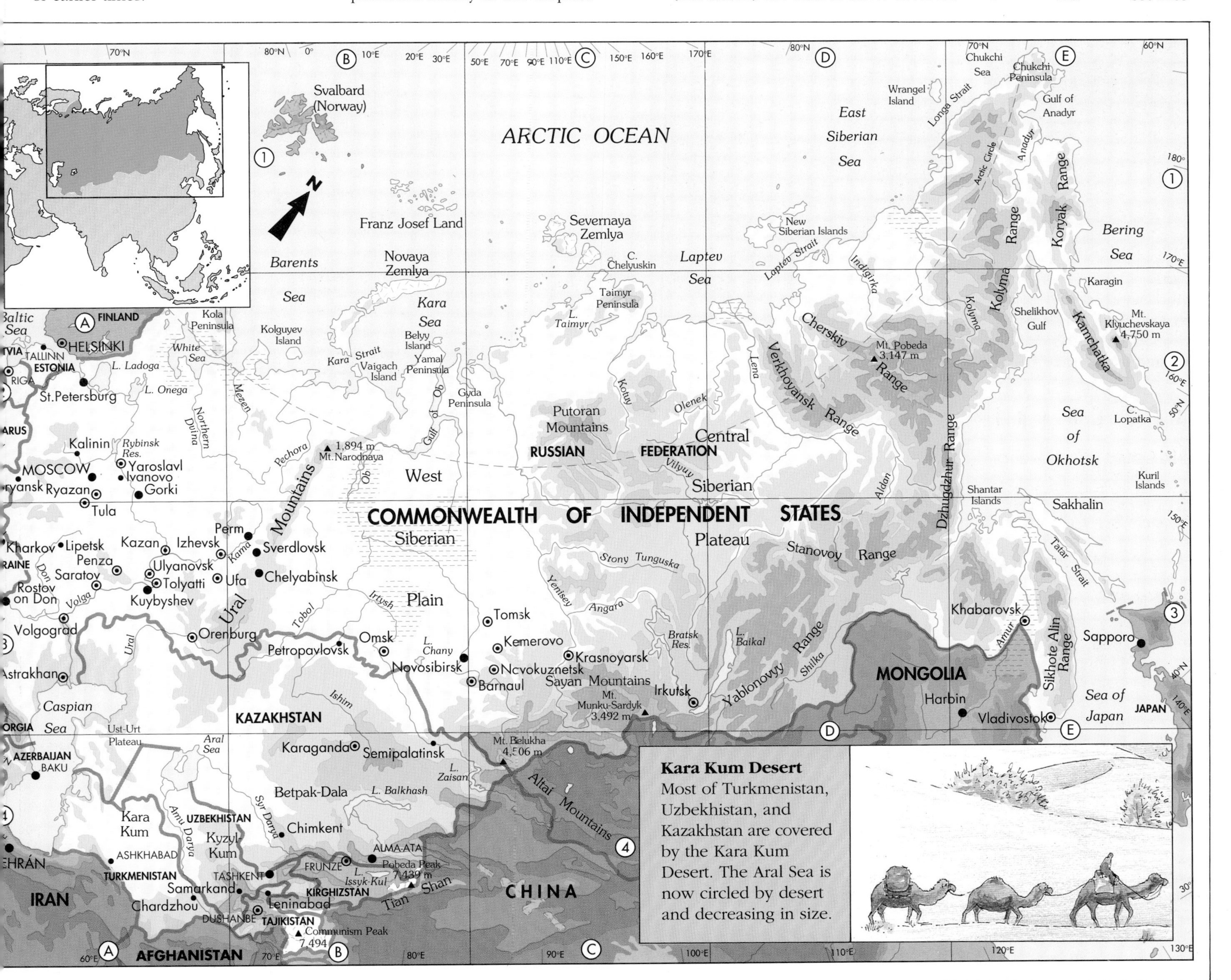

Kara Kum Desert
Most of Turkmenistan, Uzbekhistan, and Kazakhstan are covered by the Kara Kum Desert. The Aral Sea is now circled by desert and decreasing in size.

SOUTHWEST ASIA

Southwest Asia, which is sometimes called the Middle East, encompasses a variety of landscapes. They range from the sandy deserts of Saudi Arabia, to the mountains of the Hindu Kush, and the low-lying valley and wide delta of the River Indus in Pakistan.

Cultures and lifestyles vary greatly. Areas that lie within the "fertile crescent" between the Tigris and Euphrates are rich farmlands. The wealth of the Gulf countries comes from their oil. Afghanistan and Pakistan, poor countries with few resources, depend on agriculture.

Bedouin Camp
The Bedouins of the Arabian deserts are nomadic people. Many still live in tents woven from goat's hair.

Desert Wildlife
Dry scrub and desert cover vast regions. Most animals like these desert mice (see above) emerge at dusk to hunt and feed.

Muslim Religion
Islam is the religion of the Arab states. All Muslims pray five times a day, at a mosque if possible (see above).

FACT CHART

- The Pamirs, where China, India, Pakistan, and Afghanistan meet, are called the "Roof of the World." The mountains rise over 25,000 feet above sea level.
- K2, in the Karakoram Mountains, is the second highest peak in the world (28,250 feet high).
- The Khyber Pass, an important trading route between northwest Pakistan and the Kabul plain of Afghanistan, is little more than 600 feet wide for part of its length.
- The Euphrates and the Indus are the two great rivers of southwest Asia. Both of them are about 1,700 miles long.
- The United Arab Emirates (UAE), a federation of seven independent Arab states (Abu Dhabi, Dubai, Sharjah, Ras al Khaimah, Fujeira, Ajman, and Umm) is one of the richest countries in the world. Its wealth comes from oil.

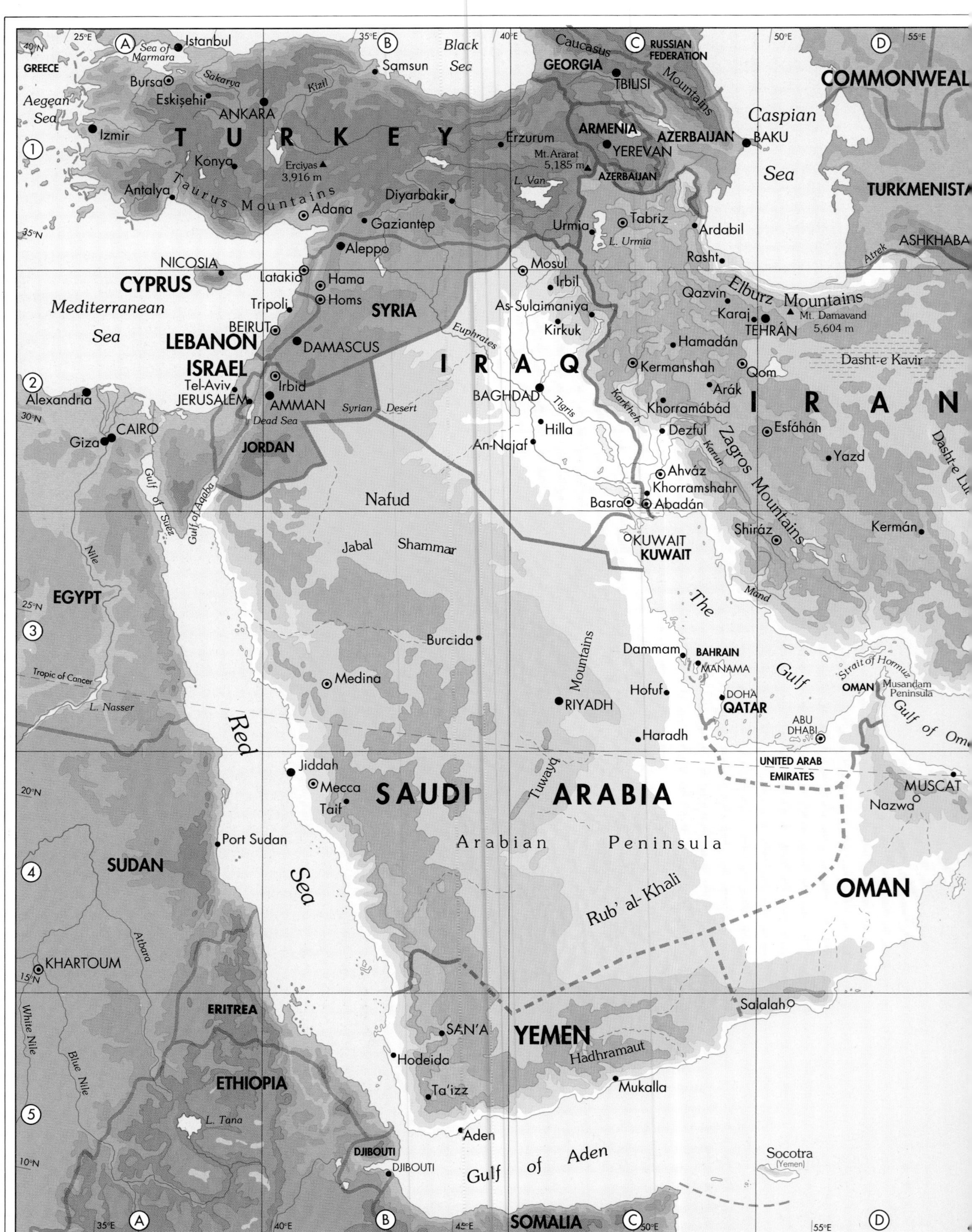

Arabian Markets

The Arabs are keen traders. Most towns have a market, or souk, where shoppers bargain for local wares. The stalls display a wide range of leather goods, brassware, pottery, jewelry, and colorful carpets. The people protect themselves from the burning sun by wearing loose clothes and headdresses (see right).

Houses for Hot Climates

These older houses in southern Iraq (see right) are very basic but are well suited to the hot climate. The flat roofs are used for drying crops or pottery in the sun. Families sometimes sleep out on the roof when the summer nights are very hot. The small windows help to keep the interior of the house cool in summer and warm in winter.

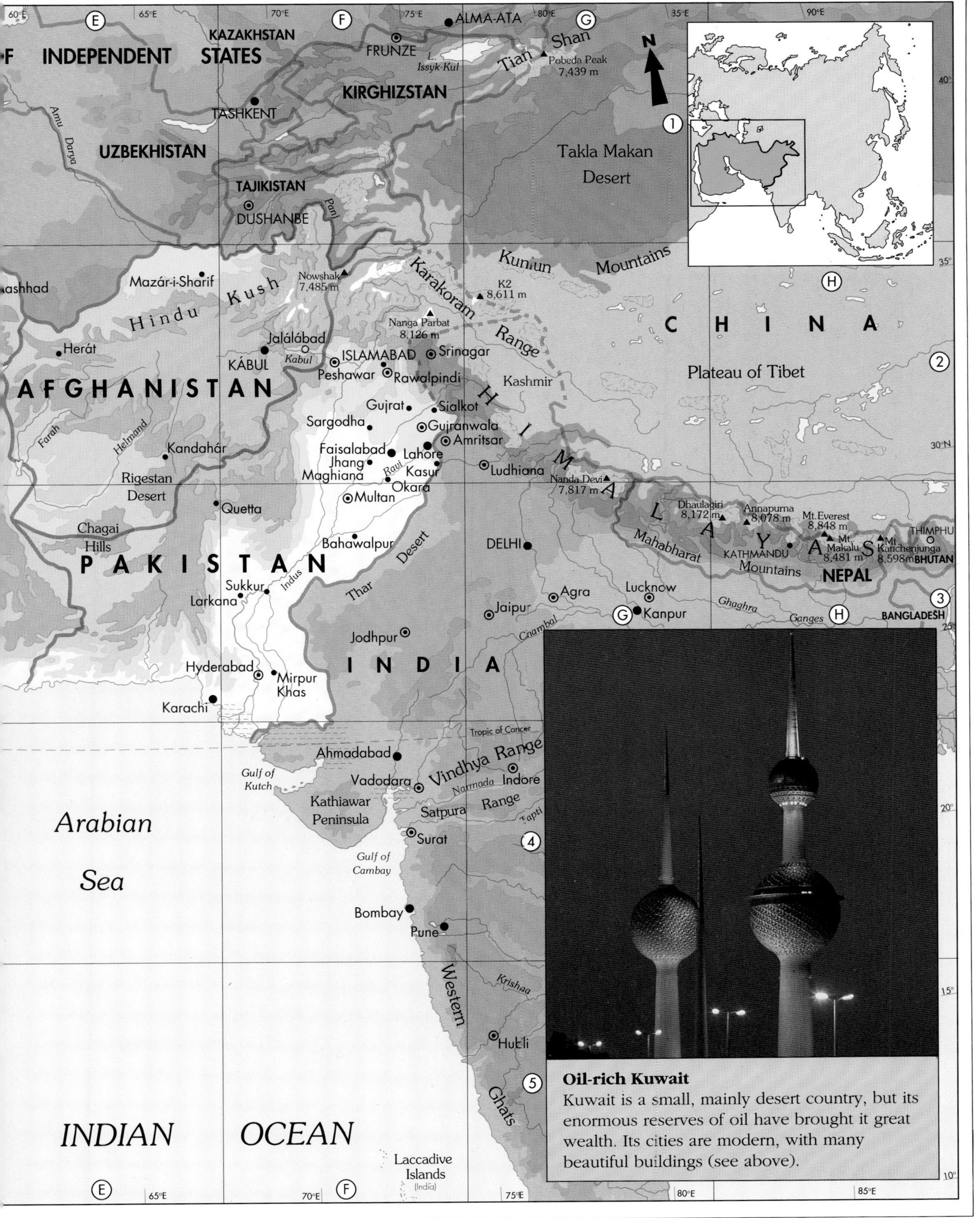

Oil-rich Kuwait

Kuwait is a small, mainly desert country, but its enormous reserves of oil have brought it great wealth. Its cities are modern, with many beautiful buildings (see above).

Ancient Skyscrapers

These buildings in Sana, in the Yemen, are more than 1,000 years old. They are built in the traditional mudbrick style, with shafts running up the center to take fresh air to each floor. The people live in extended families, so that a single building may house all the members of one family.

Family Wealth

The wealth of many Arabian families was stored as jewelry rather than money. This jewelry comes from Oman.

Scale approximately 1:15,000,000
At the scale of this map the straight line distance from Riyadh (C3) to Kabul (F2) is approximately 1,510 miles (2,431 km).

0 200 400 600 km
0 100 200 300 miles

EASTERN MEDITERRANEAN

Offshore Oilrigs
The Gulf has numerous oilrigs (see above) and is dotted with terminals, loading platforms, and refineries.

The eastern Mediterranean Sea is bordered by Turkey, Syria, Lebanon, and Israel. The fertile coastal plains, where most people live, have a mild climate. Further inland the ground rises to a plateau of steppe and then merges into hot desert.

Turkey, which is separated into two by the Bosporus, is a land of farms, scrub, steppe, and pasture. Jordan, an inland country of mostly desert plateau, has few resources. Most people live in the more fertile west and north. The beautiful island of Cyprus, consisting of two mountain ranges with a broad plain between, lies in the northeast Mediterranean.

Ancient Cities
In the Eastern Mediterranean there are many remains of ancient cities such as Palmyra in Syria (see left).

The Useful Date Palm
Date palms have been cultivated for hundreds of years, and every part of the tree is useful. Dates are one of the most important foods of the region. They are eaten fresh or dried.

FACT CHART

- The Dead Sea is the lowest point in the world – 1,300 feet *below* sea level. It is not really a sea at all, but a salt lake. It is five times as salty as the ocean.
- Agri Dagi – Mount Ararat – is the highest peak in Turkey (16,853 feet).
- Israel was founded after World War 2 as a home for the Jewish people. Over a million Jews from all over the world have settled there since 1948.
- The Bosporus, which means "ox ford" is a short narrow strait that separates Europe from Asia Minor. It is 18 miles long and less than half a mile wide at its narrowest point.

Scale approximately 1:7,895,000
At the scale of this map the straight line distance from Istanbul (A1) to Jerusalem (C3) is approximately 727 miles (1,170 km).

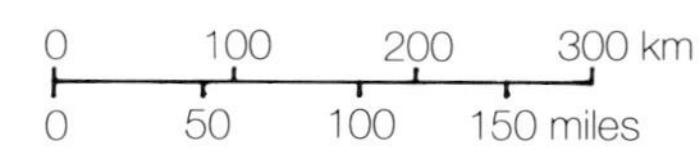

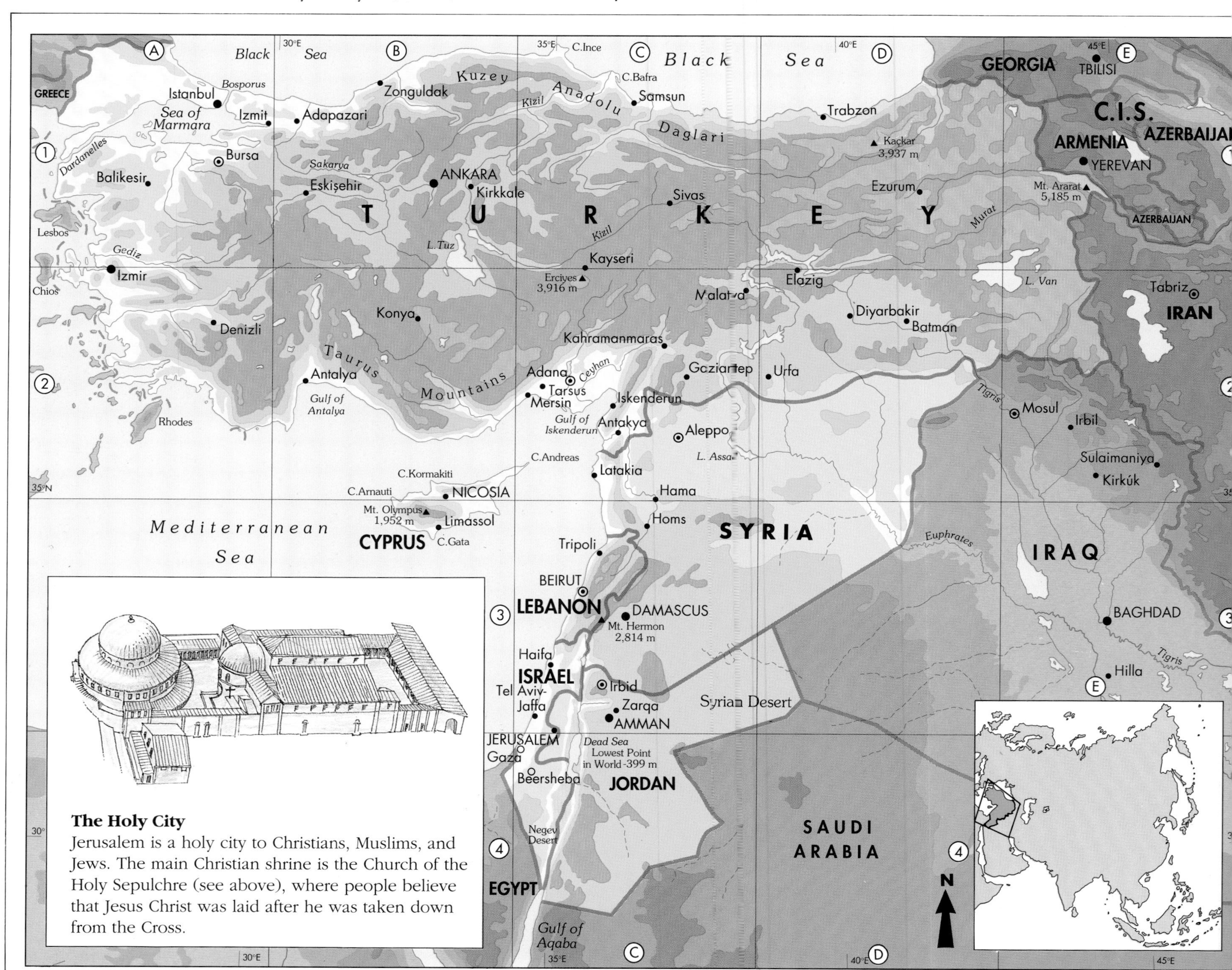

The Holy City
Jerusalem is a holy city to Christians, Muslims, and Jews. The main Christian shrine is the Church of the Holy Sepulchre (see above), where people believe that Jesus Christ was laid after he was taken down from the Cross.

THE GULF

Cool Clothes
Many people in the region wear loose-fitting robes and headdresses. They protect people from the sun and dust and keep them cool.

FACT CHART

- The Ghawar oilfield in Saudi Arabia is the world's largest. It has twice as much oil as the entire reserves of the United States.
- In addition to the enormous reserves of oil, the Gulf region has nearly 25 percent of the world's natural gas reserves.
- Bahrain is a group of islands 20 miles off the east coast of the Gulf. The largest island is only 30 miles long and about 10 miles wide.
- The Middle East now produces about 10 million barrels of oil a day (one barrel is about 35 gallons).

Scale approximately 1:7,500,000
At the scale of this map the straight line distance from Kuwait (B2) to Abu Dhabi (D3) is approximately 520 miles (837 km).

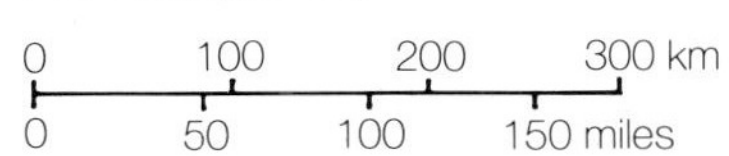

The Gulf is the arm of the Arabian Sea that lies between the deserts of Arabia and Iran. It is about 600 miles long and 200 miles wide, narrowing to 50 miles at the Strait of Hormuz, where it connects with the Gulf of Oman. The great rivers, the Tigris and the Euphrates, reach the Gulf at its northern end.

The Gulf is very shallow, with an average depth of only 330 feet. Its waters are warm, sometimes reaching 95°F in the summer. Once famous for its pearl-bearing oysters, its vast oil reserves are now commercially much more important. The Gulf states derive their wealth from exporting oil to Europe, Japan, and North America.

Local Fishing
Fish are an important resource in the Gulf. Commercial trawlers are usually used, but some of the local people still use the traditional *dhow* (see right).

Istanbul
Istanbul (see below) is Turkey's chief port and center of trade. It lies on the shores of the Bosporus.

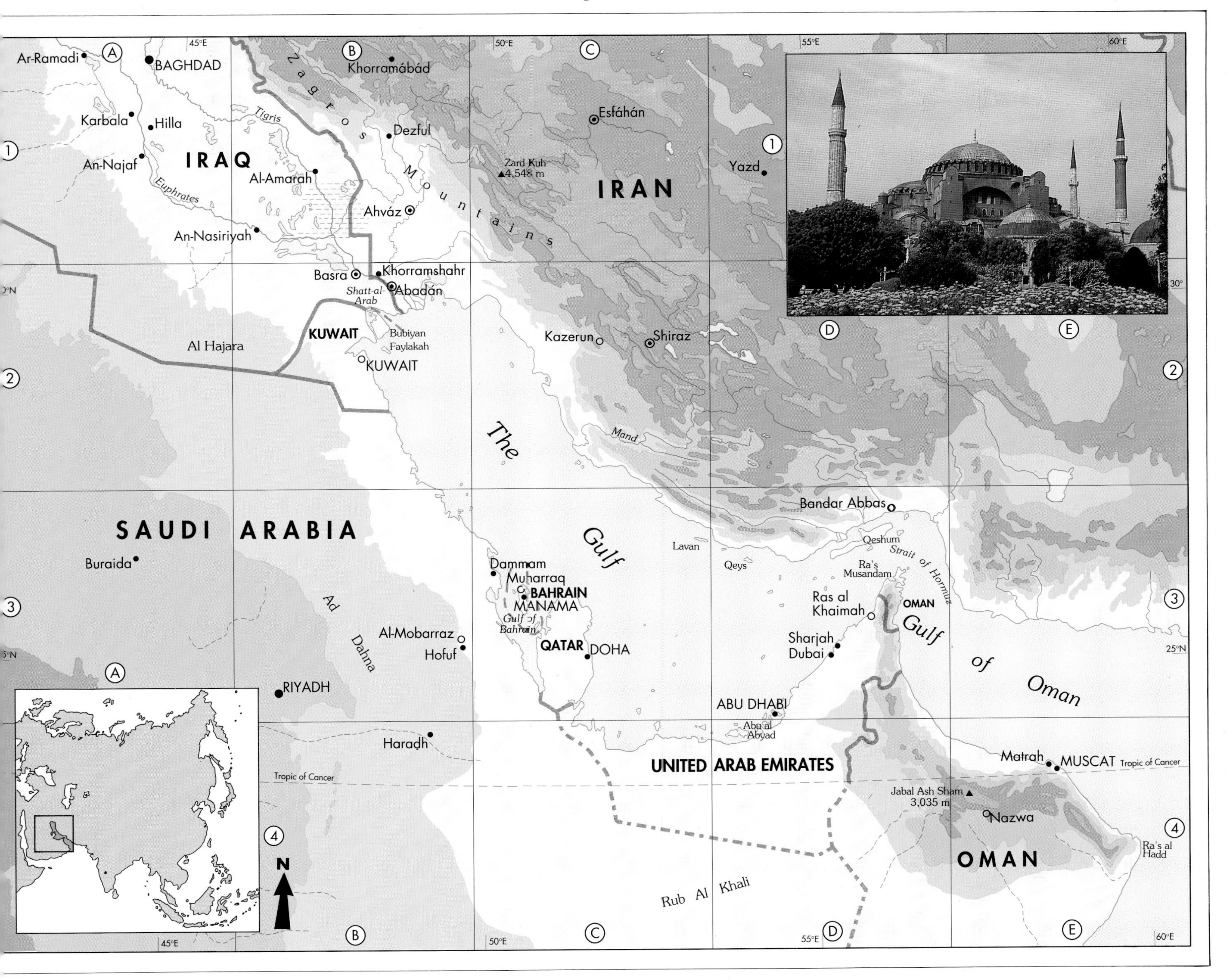

SOUTH ASIA

Over one billion people live in southern Asia. Most of them are farmers who live on the wetter coasts and in the fertile plains.

India, the largest country in South Asia, is a flat plateau, with mountain ranges on the east and west coasts and to the north. The Thar Desert lies to the west. Bangladesh, consisting of the flat, fertile floodplain of the Ganges, is dramatically affected by the annual monsoon.

Mount Everest
Mount Everest (see below) lies on Nepal's border with China. At 29,028 feet, it is the world's highest mountain.

Ancient Temples
The Hindu temples at Petua in northwest Bangladesh were built around 1,200 years ago.

The Lotus Flower
The pink-flowered lotus, a native to South Asia, is sacred to the Hindus.

Indian Tiger
Tigers are found in many areas of Asia. There are more Indian tigers (see above) than any other kind in the wild.

FACT CHART

- Around 871 million people live in India – 16 percent of the world's population.
- The Kingdom of Bhutan has a small population of about 1 1/2 million. Only 9,000 people live in Thimphu, the capital.
- The Ganges, South Asia's longest river, rises in a Himalayan ice cave and flows 1,550 miles to the floodplain of Bangladesh.
- India has two monsoon winds – the southwest brings rain from June to September; the northeast blows from October to February.
- India has 25 main languages and more than 1,600 local languages.

Scale approximately 1:15,957,000
At the scale of this map the straight line distance from Kathmandu (C2) to Colombo (B5) is approximately 1,473 miles (2,372 km).

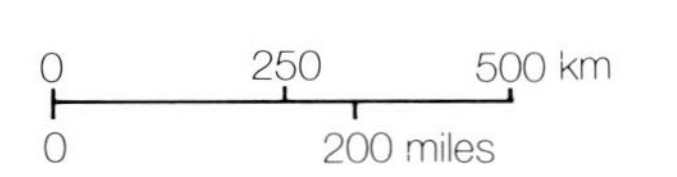

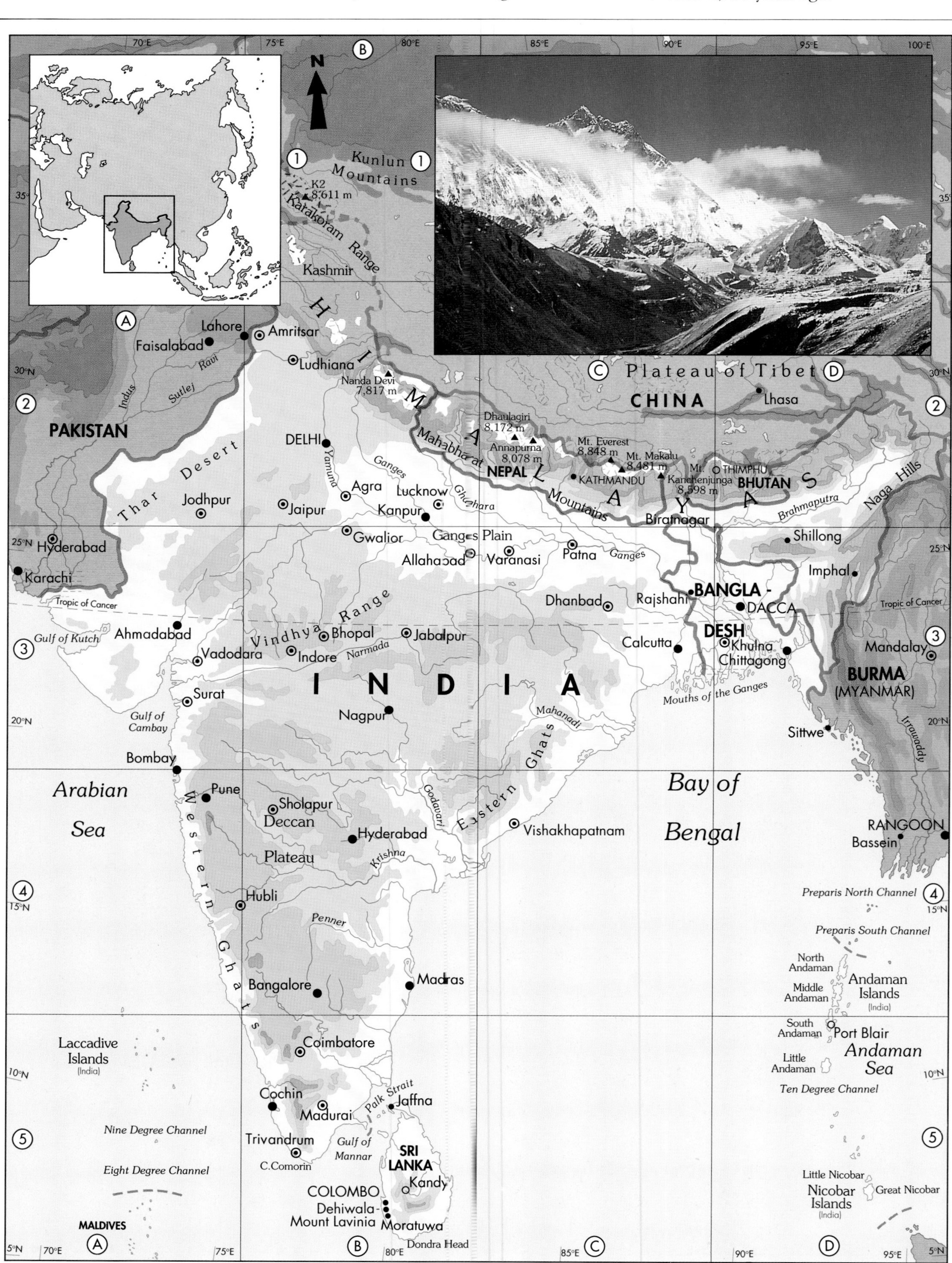

INDOCHINA

Tropical Fruit
The hot, wet climate is ideal for growing tropical fruits (see above).

The lands of Indochina – Burma (Myanmar), Thailand, Laos, Cambodia (Kampuchea), and Vietnam – are mountainous. Burma, bordered by mountains to the west, north, and east, has a tropical climate with evergreen rain forests, lush mangrove swamps, and monsoon forests.

The mountains of Thailand and Laos are thickly forested. Many of the people make their living from forestry. Cambodia and Vietnam are mainly agricultural.

Laos
The triumphal arch in Vientiane, the capital of Laos, is a famous landmark (see below).

Natural Resources
Some of the world's finest gemstones, including rubies, jade, and silver, are mined in the mountains of Burma.

Classical Dance
Classical dancers from Sri Lanka, Thailand (see above), and Indonesia train from childhood to perform the country's traditional stories. Dance dramas are frequently performed at Hindu and Buddhist festivals.

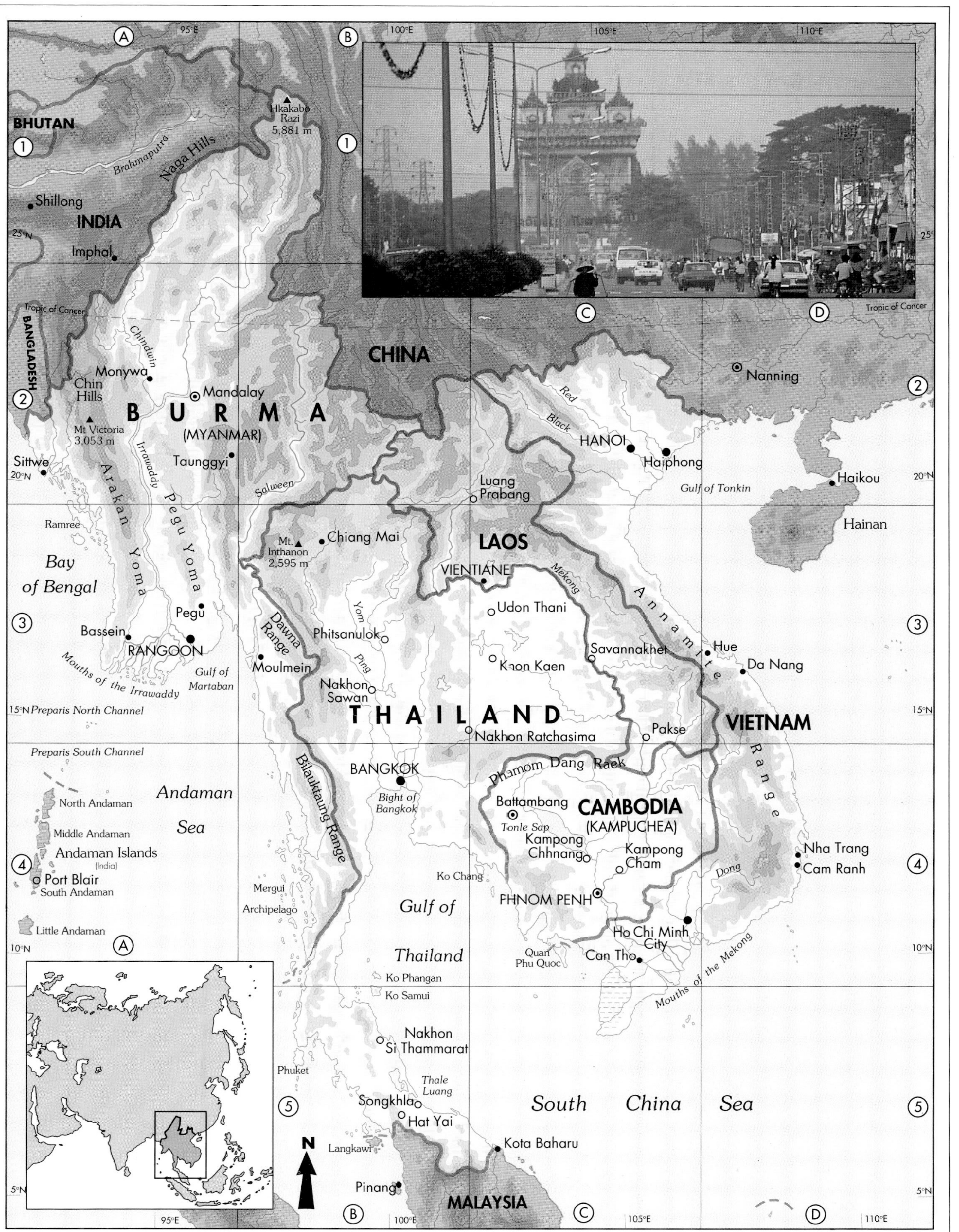

FACT CHART

- The Mekong is the major river of Indochina. It rises in the Tibetan mountains and flows southwards for 2,600 miles through Laos and Cambodia to southern Vietnam.
- Burma's highest peak is Mount Hkakabo at 19,578 feet above sea level.
- The River Irrawaddy flows for 1,300 miles through the heart of Burma. The delta is a vast paddy field nearly 200 miles wide.
- The Red and Mekong River deltas in Vietnam are less than 10 feet above sea level – they are the main farming areas.
- The Kohne Falls on the Mekong River in Laos are a series of rapids 6 miles long.

Scale approximately 1:11,538,500
At the scale of this map the straight line distance from Hanoi (C2) to Songkla (B5) is approximately 1,000 miles (1,610 km).

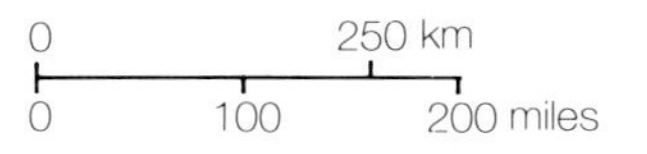

SOUTHEAST ASIA

Southeast Asia is a complex mixture of modern trading nations and traditional farming communities. Its tropical rain forests and mangrove swamps are a haven for wildlife.

Malaysia has two distinct regions – 80 percent of the population lives on the Malay Peninsula and the rest in the states of Sarawak and Sabah, on the island of Borneo.

Indonesia is composed of hundreds of tropical islands in the Pacific and Indian Oceans. This vast area is subject to severe earthquakes and has many volcanoes.

The Spice Trade
Centuries ago, Arab merchants used to bring spices to Europe from the Moluccas, a large group of islands also known as The Spice Islands. Nutmeg, mace (see above), cinnamon, cloves, and pepper are still the traditional crops.

Kuala Lumpur
Kuala Lumpur (see above), the capital of Malaysia and the seat of government, is a mixture of ancient and modern buildings.

Singapore
Singapore is an important center for trade and finance, and one of the world's busiest ports (see above).

Scale approximately 1:13,636,000
At the scale of this map the straight line distance from Singapore (B3) to Balikpapan (D4) is approximately 915 miles (1,473 km).

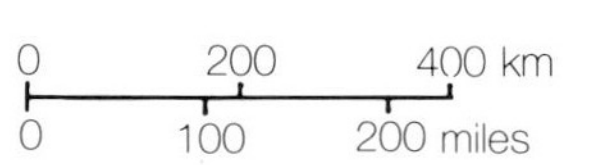

Disappearing Wildlife
Every year, vast areas of Asian forests are cut down for timber or cleared for farming. This means that natural habitats for numerous plants and animals like the giant hornbill (see left) and the orangutan of Borneo (see right) are being destroyed. Many of the local people who opposed the logging of the forests have lost their homes.

Houses on Stilts
In Southeast Asia houses are often built on stilts to protect them from floods caused by the monsoon. Along the coasts and around the islands whole fishing villages are built on stilts and can only be reached by boat. The houses are connected to each other by a series of floats (see left).

Terraces of Rice
In the Philippines, rice is still grown on terraces that have been in use for over 3,000 years. The supply of water is carefully controlled so that two or even three crops a year are possible (see left).

FACT CHART

- The highest peak in the Philippines is Mount Apo (9,692 feet); the largest lake is Laguna de Bay (356 square miles).
- Krakatoa, an island volcano between Sumatra and Java, exploded in 1883 in one of the greatest eruptions ever recorded.
- Singapore is one of the most densely populated places with almost 3 million people.
- Indonesia has over 13,600 islands and has more active volcanoes than anywhere else.
- Borneo is one of the hottest and wettest places in the world.
- Nearly 75 percent of tropical hardwoods come from Asia.
- As much as 5 feet of rain falls during the monsoon.
- Puncak Jaya (16,503 feet) in Irian Jaya is the highest peak.
- The Philippines has over 7,000 islands.

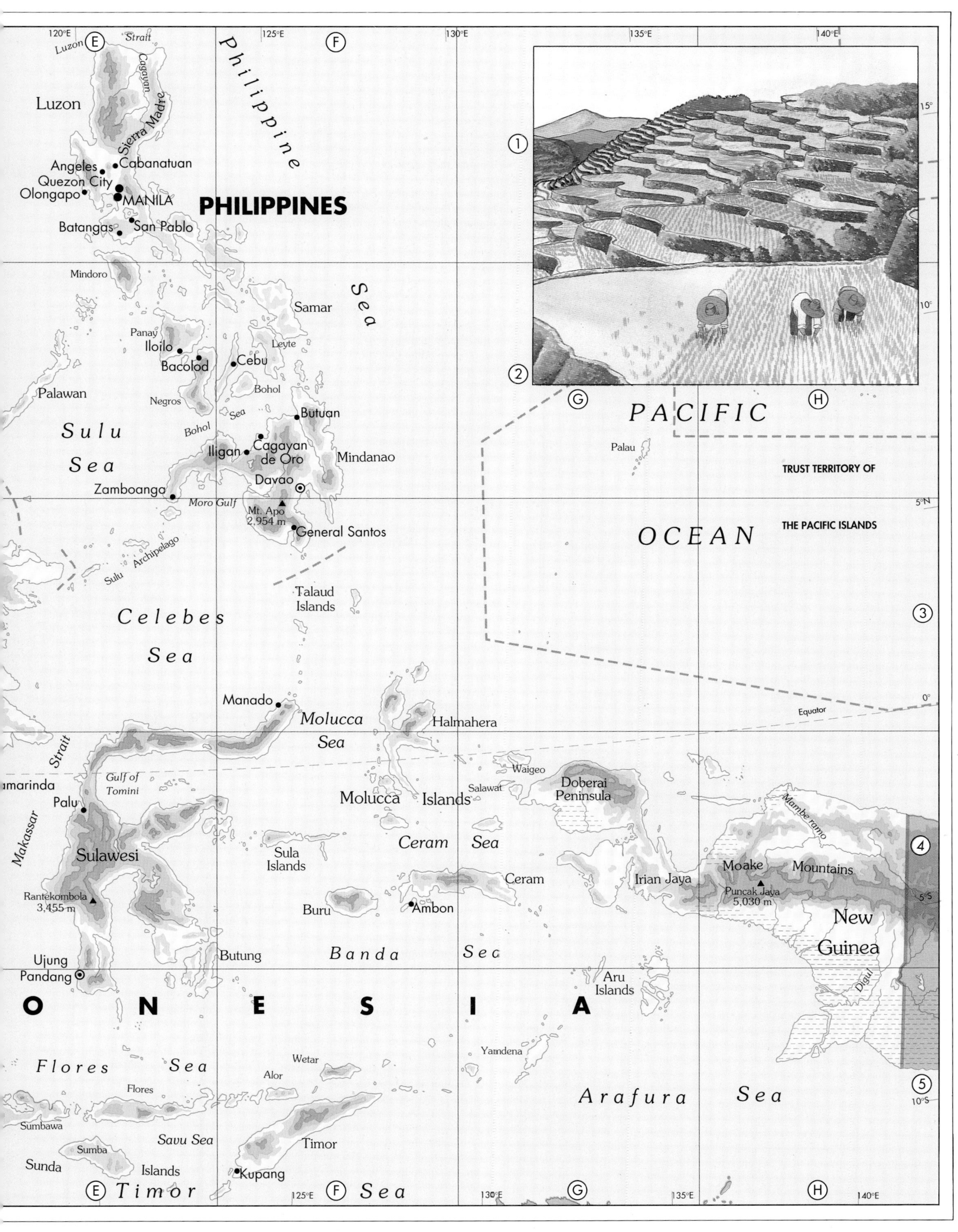

Brunei
Brunei lies on the north coast of the island of Borneo. The wealth produced from oil deposits means that most people have a high standard of living and food is plentiful (see above).

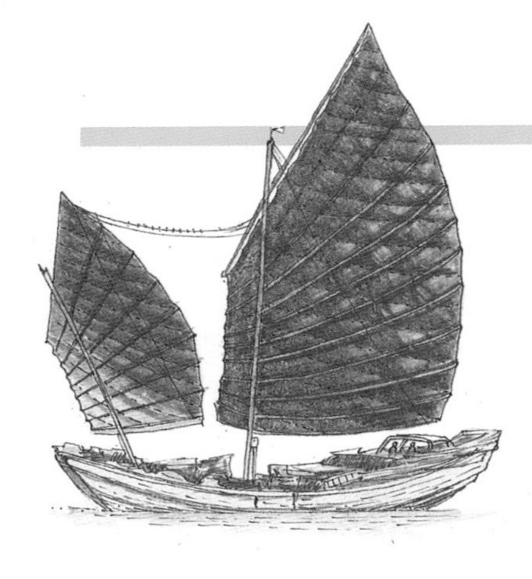

East Asia is dominated by China, the third largest country in the world. There are great variations in its landscape. The Tibetan highlands are a cold plateau bordered by towering mountains, whereas the fertile Southern Uplands have a tropical climate.

Mongolia is a high plateau rising to mountains in the west with the "singing sands" of the Gobi Desert in the south.

To the east lie Korea and the volcanic islands of Japan and Taiwan. These are some of the most industrialized nations in the world.

Traditional Boats
Traditional Chinese junks are still used for fishing in the coastal waters, though today most of them have motors as well as sails.

Buddhism
Buddhism reached China and Japan from India. About one in five of all the people in the world follow the teachings of Buddha.

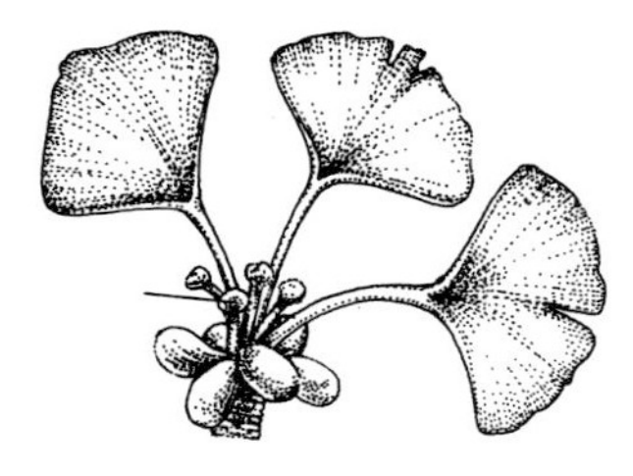

Ancient Trees
Wild ginkgo, or maidenhair, trees grow in one tiny area of China. They are grown for their fruits, timber, and oil.

The Great Wall of China
The Great Wall of China is about 1,500 miles long. Built to keep out warring Tatar tribes, it was completed in 214 BC.

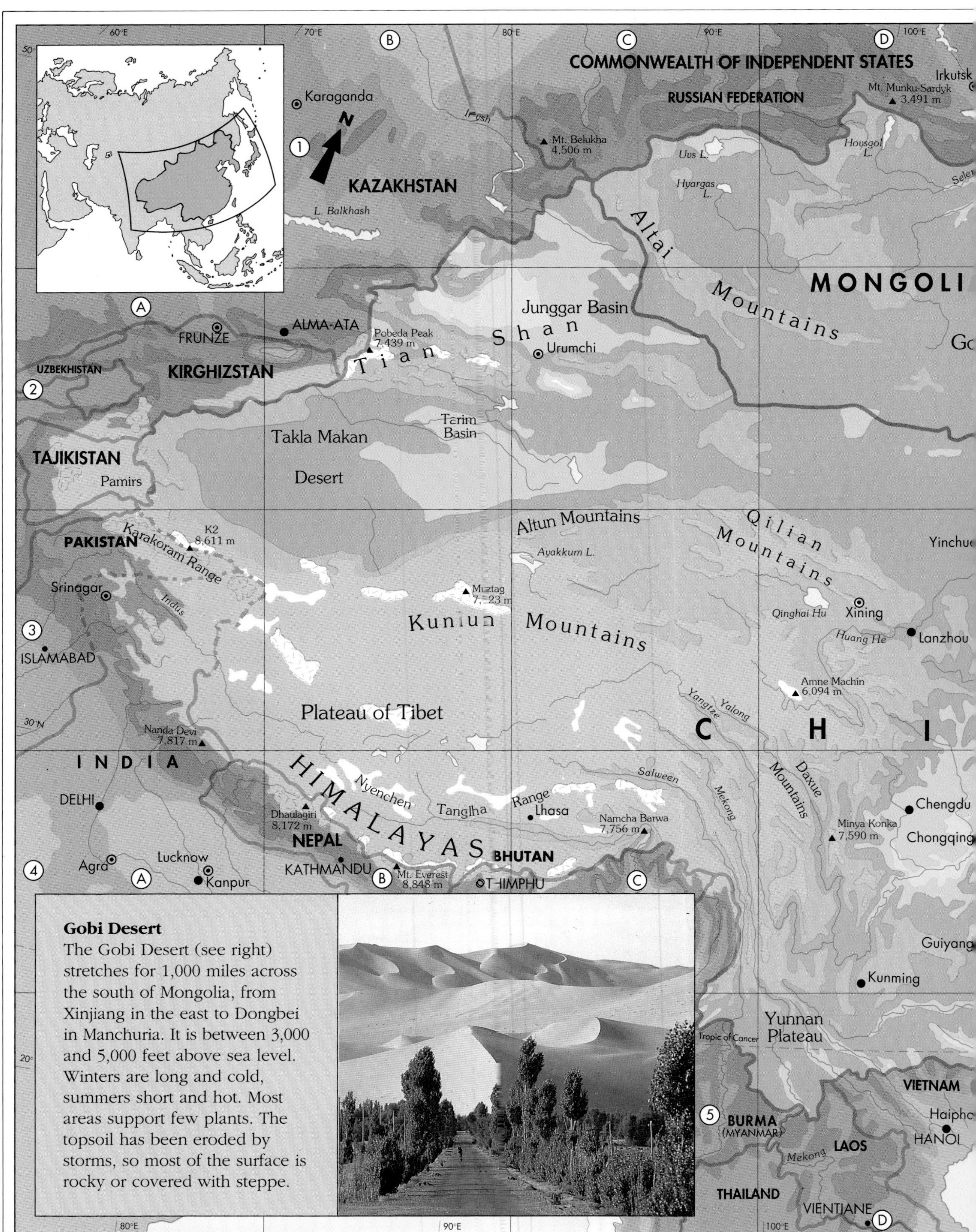

Gobi Desert
The Gobi Desert (see right) stretches for 1,000 miles across the south of Mongolia, from Xinjiang in the east to Dongbei in Manchuria. It is between 3,000 and 5,000 feet above sea level. Winters are long and cold, summers short and hot. Most areas support few plants. The topsoil has been eroded by storms, so most of the surface is rocky or covered with steppe.

Potala Palace
Potala Palace at Lhasa was built for the Dalai Lama. He was the Supreme Ruler of Tibet until China invaded in 1950.

Panda
The giant panda lives high in the mountains of southwestern China and eastern Tibet. It is now endangered and 12 panda reserves have been set up to protect these delightful creatures.

The World's Largest City
Tokyo, the capital of Japan, is the world's largest city. It has a population of over 25 million (see left).

Seoul
Seoul, the capital of South Korea, has spread far outside the ancient walls with their eight gateways (see below).

FACT CHART

- The Yangtze, China's longest river and the third longest in the world, flows 3,400 miles from Tibet to the East China Sea.
- The Huang He flows for 2,900 miles from the Kunlun Mountains to the Yellow Sea.
- Fujiyama, at 12,388 feet, is the highest peak in Japan. The last eruption of this volcano was in 1707.
- China's population is about 1,115,883,000 – over 20 percent of the world's total.
- Japan's islands average 1,500 earthquakes a year, but most are only slight tremors. There are also 150 volcanoes, of which 60 are active.
- Japan has the world's longest railway tunnel under the mountains – the Oshimuzu tunnel (nearly 14 miles long).
- China's Grand Canal is about 1,118 miles long and can carry ships of up to 2,200 tons.
- The highest peak in North Korea is Mount Paektu-san (9,003 feet). Mount Halla-san (6,398 feet), an extinct volcano, is the highest in South Korea.

Scale approximately 1:16,667,000
At the scale of this map the straight line distance from Hong Kong (E5) to Tokyo (H3) is approximately 1,797 miles (2,893 km).

0 250 500 km
0 150 300 miles

OCEANIA

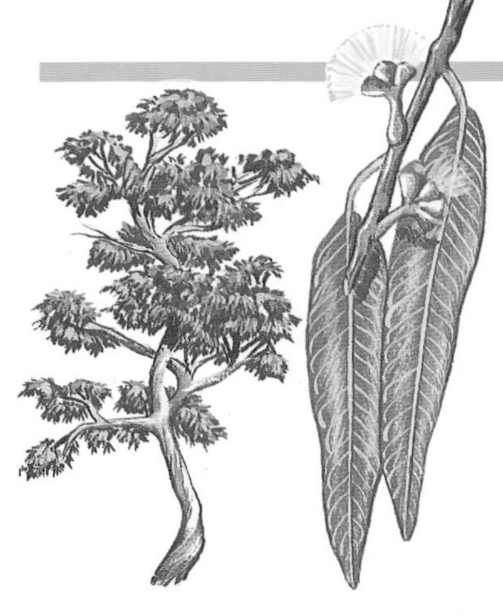

Oceania takes its name from the Pacific Ocean, the vast expanse of water that lies between Asia and the Americas. The continent is often called Australasia. Australia, a land of forests, deserts, and scrub, is the largest country in the region. It has a unique wildlife.

To the north, across the Torres Strait, lies Papua-New Guinea, a land of remote mountains and tropical forests. The twin islands of New Zealand lie to the southeast of Australia. Thousands of other tiny islands are scattered eastwards across the Pacific.

Gum Trees
The Sydney blue gum tree is one of the many eucalyptus trees of Australia. These tall, broadleaved evergreens provide timber and oil.

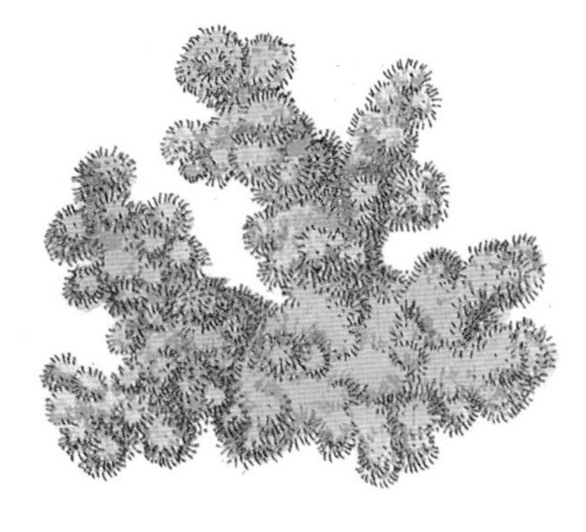

Coral Reefs
The northeastern coast of Australia is shielded by the world's largest expanse of coral. This Great Barrier Reef is 1,256 miles long.

FACT CHART

- Australasia is the smallest continent covering only 6 percent of the earth.
- The original inhabitants of Oceania include the Aborigines of Australia, and the Melanesians, Micronesians, and Polynesians of the Pacific islands. The Maoris of New Zealand are just one of the many Polynesian peoples.
- The highest point in the region is Mount Wilhelm (14,793 feet) in Papua-New Guinea.
- Lake Eyre in Australia is the largest lake in the region (3,436 square miles).
- The oldest known rocks (4,300 million years) come from near Perth.
- In ancient times the inhabitants of Oceania were the world's greatest seafarers. The Lapita people, ancestors of today's islanders, settled almost 8 million square miles of the Pacific between about 1500 BC and AD 1000. They used sailing canoes.

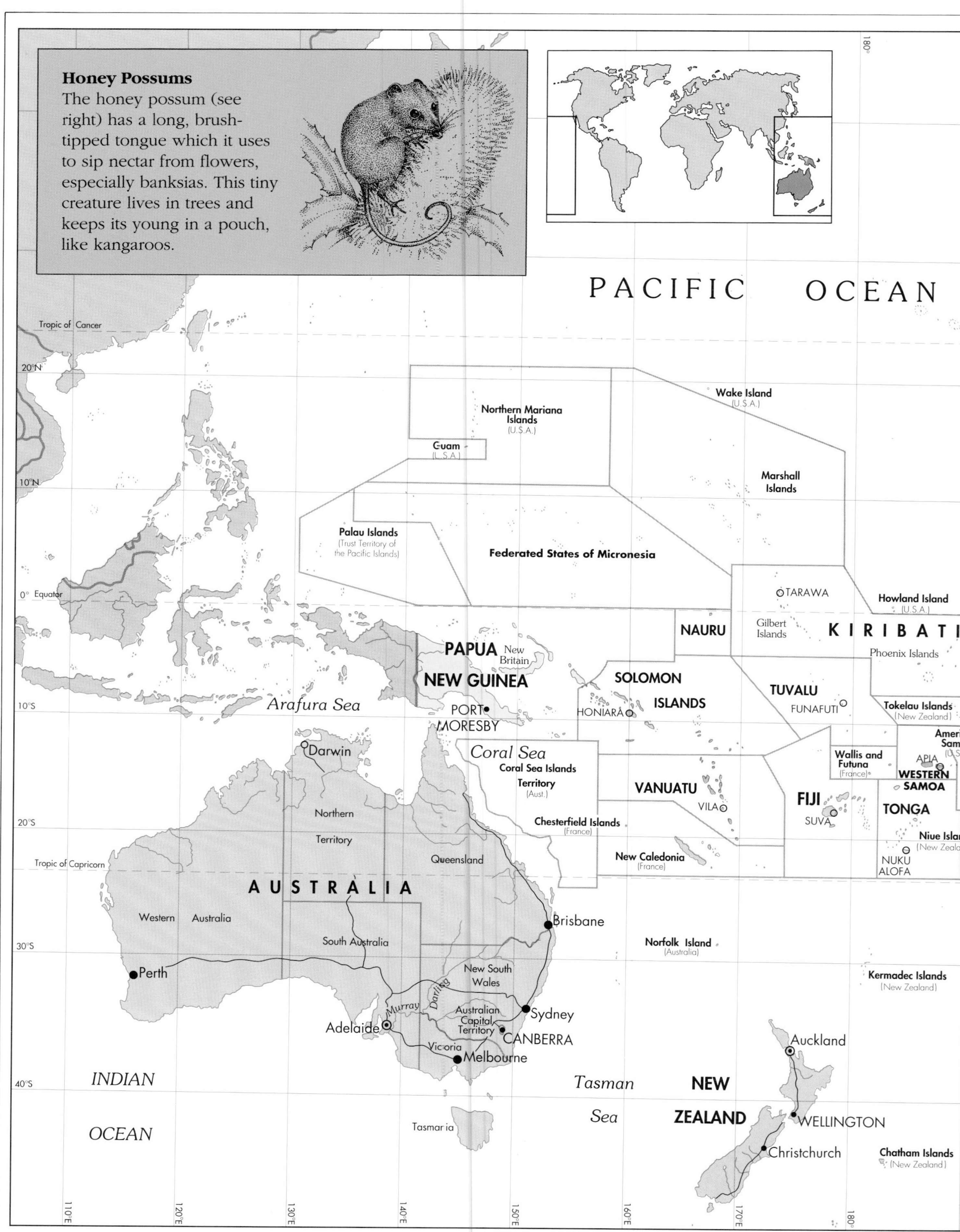

Honey Possums
The honey possum (see right) has a long, brush-tipped tongue which it uses to sip nectar from flowers, especially banksias. This tiny creature lives in trees and keeps its young in a pouch, like kangaroos.

Strange Nature
The platypus (see left) is a strange-looking creature that lives in Australian rivers. It belongs to a small group of mammals, called monotremes, which lay eggs. Australia has many unique mammals. Some, such as kangaroos, koalas, and wombats, are marsupials. Their young are protected by a special pouch on the bodies of their mothers.

The Great Dividing Range
The main mountain range runs down eastern Australia from Queensland to Victoria. This range (see left) includes the beautiful Australian Alps and the Blue Mountains. There are smaller ranges in Australia, but none of them is over 5,000 feet.

160°W 150°W 140°W 130°W

40°N

30°N

Tropic of Cancer

Hawaiian Islands (U.S.A)

20°N

10°N

Line Islands

Equator 0°

Caroline Islands

Marquesas Islands (France)

10°S

Cook Islands (New Zealand)

Tuamotu Archipelago (France)

Society Islands (France)

French Polynesia (France)

Tubuai Islands (France)

20°S

Tropic of Capricorn

Pitcairn Island (United Kingdom)

(U.K.)

30°S

40°S

160°W 150°W 140°W 130°W

Number of people per square kilometer
- 10-100
- 2-10
- less than 2

Population
The total population of Australia is about 17 million; most people live in the southeast. There are almost 12 million people living on the Pacific Islands.

- Tundra/Mountain
- Mixed/Broadleaf Forest
- Scrub
- Grassland
- Tropical Rain Forest
- Tropical Forest
- Desert

- Oceanic
- Subtropical – humid
- Subtropical – wet and dry
- Tropical – humid
- Tropical – wet and dry
- Arid
- High Altitude

Natural Vegetation and Climate
There is a wide range of vegetation in Oceania from dry deserts to tropical jungles.

New Zealand Southern Beech
New Zealand has almost 17 million acres of forest. The 90-feet-high southern beech grows in the wetter regions.

Pacific Islands
Most Pacific islands are formed from volcanic rock and coral. Many of the local people, like this woman at a cultural center in Fiji, practice traditional crafts.

Scale approximately 1:48,550,000

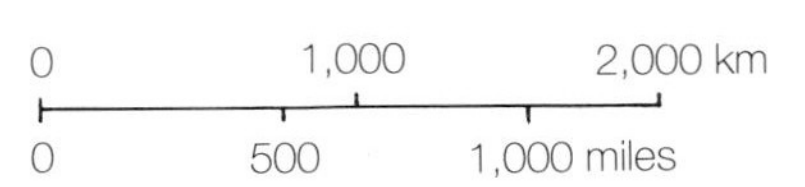

AUSTRALIA

Australia is the sixth largest country in the world. It is mostly a land of burning deserts and dry scrub. In the far east there are more fertile regions, where crops are grown and cattle and sheep raised. It is in this area that the largest cities have grown up.

Australia is divided into six states and two territories. The national capital is at Canberra, but the largest city is Sydney, in New South Wales.

Australia's First Inhabitants
Many Aborigines, the first settlers in Australia, still try to follow the ancient traditions of their people.

Wildlife
Because of Australia's long isolation from other lands, it has many unique animals. Kangaroos (see above) and kookaburras (see below) are celebrated in Australian folk songs and tales.

City Skyline
Australia's finest modern building is the Sydney Opera House (see below), which overlooks a beautiful harbor.

FACT CHART

- The Murray-Darling (2,330 miles) is the longest river.
- Cloncurry in Queensland holds Australia's temperature record – 127.6°F.
- Only 13 percent of Australia is above 1,640 feet high. The highest point is Mount Kosciusko at over 7,300 feet.
- Australia's Great Barrier Reef, the largest in the world, stretches 1,256 miles along the coast and is over 1,650 feet thick.

Scale approximately 1:23,530,000
At the scale of this map the straight line distance from Perth (A4) to Brisbane (D3) is approximately 2,237 miles (3,600 km).

0 400 800 km
0 200 400 miles

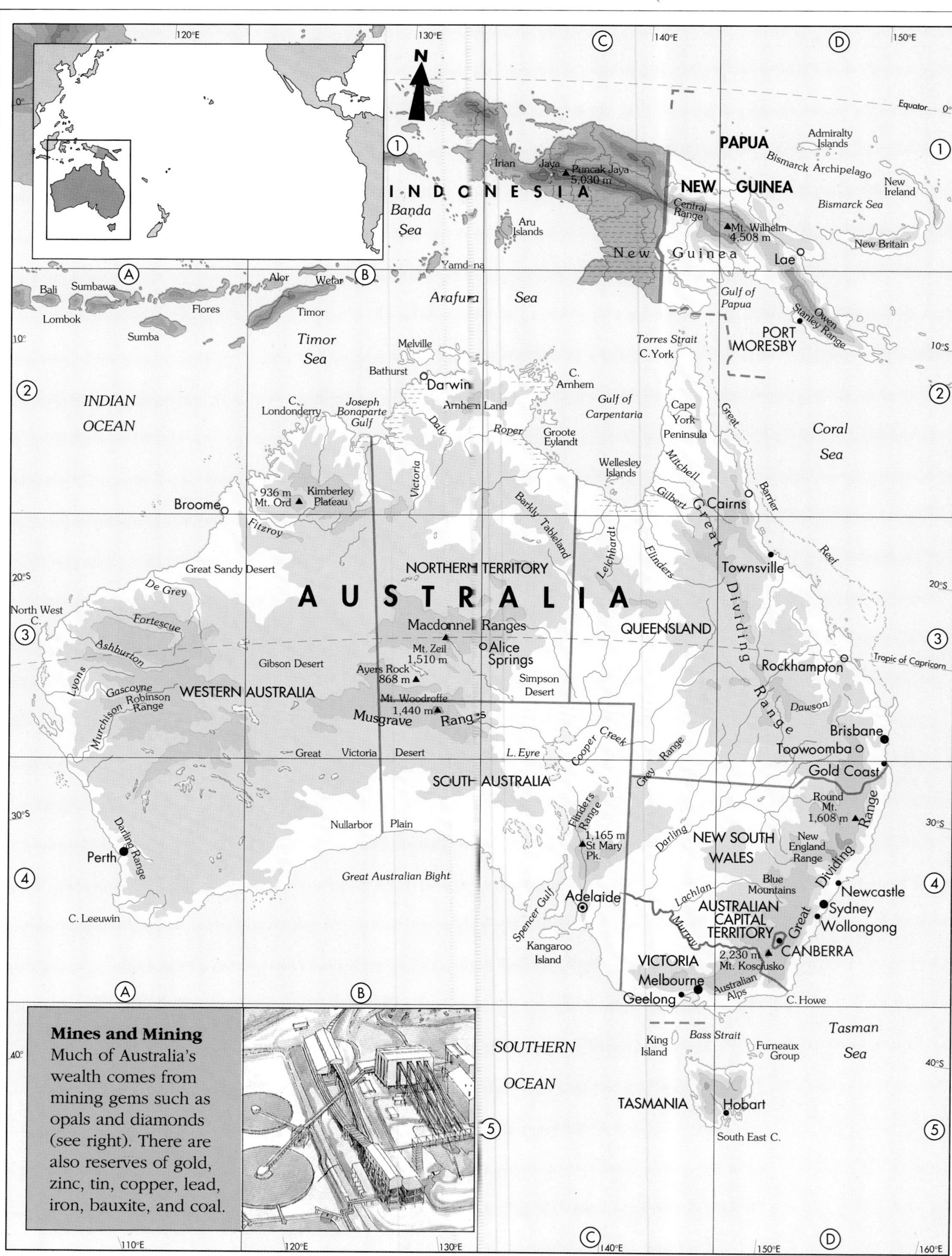

Mines and Mining
Much of Australia's wealth comes from mining gems such as opals and diamonds (see right). There are also reserves of gold, zinc, tin, copper, lead, iron, bauxite, and coal.

NEW ZEALAND

Sheep Farming
For each human being in New Zealand, there are 20 sheep! The countryside provides ideal pasture, and New Zealand is famous for its lamb.

New Zealand consists of two major islands – North Island and South Island – and several smaller ones. A mountain range, the Southern Alps, run the length of South Island with flat, fertile plains stretching to the east coast.

North Island has fertile grazing land and a central plateau with active volcanoes. Sheep and dairy farming provide the main exports. Forestry and fishing are becoming increasingly important industries.

The Tuatara
The tuatara (see right) is the only reptile of its kind to survive into modern times. It lives only on offshore islands.

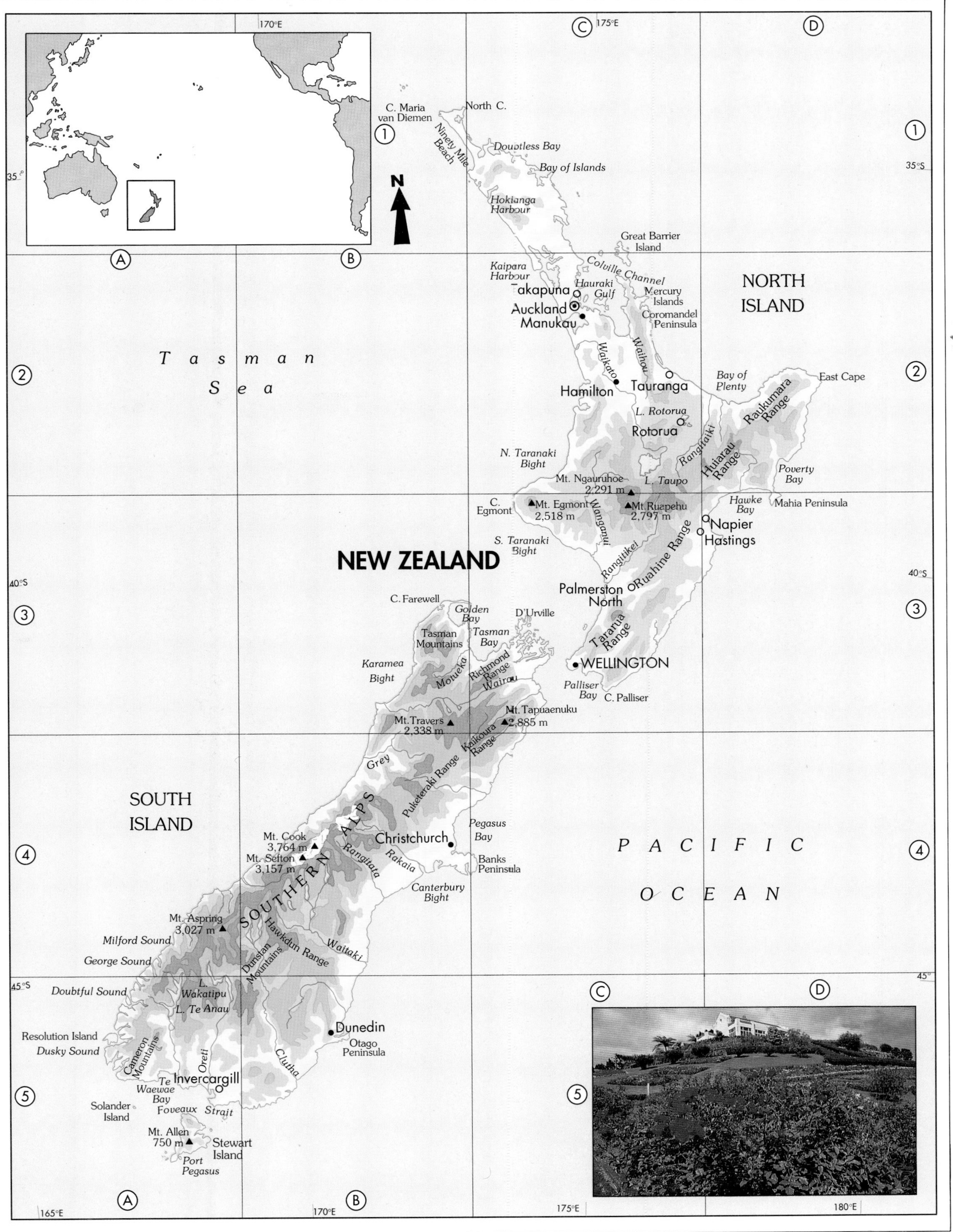

Kauri Forests
The lowlands of North Island support forests of kauri pines. These trees can grow to be 150 feet high with a diameter of up to 23 feet. Their gummy resin is used in varnishes. Some of these pines are 4,000 years old.

FACT CHART

- Twenty peaks of the Southern Alps exceed 10,000 feet – the highest is Mount Cook (12,352 feet).
- The kiwi – an unusual flightless bird – is the national symbol of New Zealand.

- Lake Taupo (234 square miles) is the largest lake.
- The Waikato River (264 miles) is the longest river.
- The Maoris, the first settlers, probably arrived in New Zealand about 1,000 years ago.

A Green Land
New Zealand's climate is ideal for growing a multitude of flowers (see left).

Scale approximately 1:6,666,000
At the scale of this map the straight line distance from Auckland (C2) to Dunedin (B5) is approximately 445 miles (717 km).

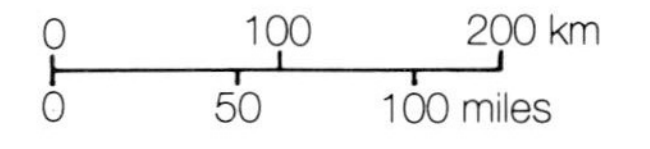

Rain Forests in Danger
The extensive rain forests of Brazil are being threatened by loggers, farmers, and road builders.

San Francisco
The cosmopolitan city of San Francisco is the financial and cultural center of the western states (see below).

The landmass of the Americas stretches from the ice floes of the Arctic Ocean to the wild, windswept wilderness of Cape Horn. It forms two very different continents joined only by a narrow strip of land, the Isthmus of Panama.

The lands in between vary from rolling grasslands, great mountain ranges, and tropical forests to deserts. They include some of the richest and some of the poorest nations on Earth. The gleaming skyscrapers of Toronto or New York City in North America contrast with the flimsy shacks of shanty towns of Mexico City and Rio de Janeiro.

Native American peoples crossed into the continent from Siberia perhaps 15,000 or more years ago. They slowly settled throughout the continent. Great civilizations developed in Mexico and in the Andes, over thousands of years.

From the 1500s onwards, Europeans began to explore and colonize the land. Today, the Americas are home to a great mixture of cultures from all over the world.

The Canadian Rockies
The mighty range of the Rocky Mountains (see right) runs through British Columbia and Alberta before crossing the United States border.

Scale approximately 1:48,550,000

0 1,000 2,000 km
0 500 1,000 miles

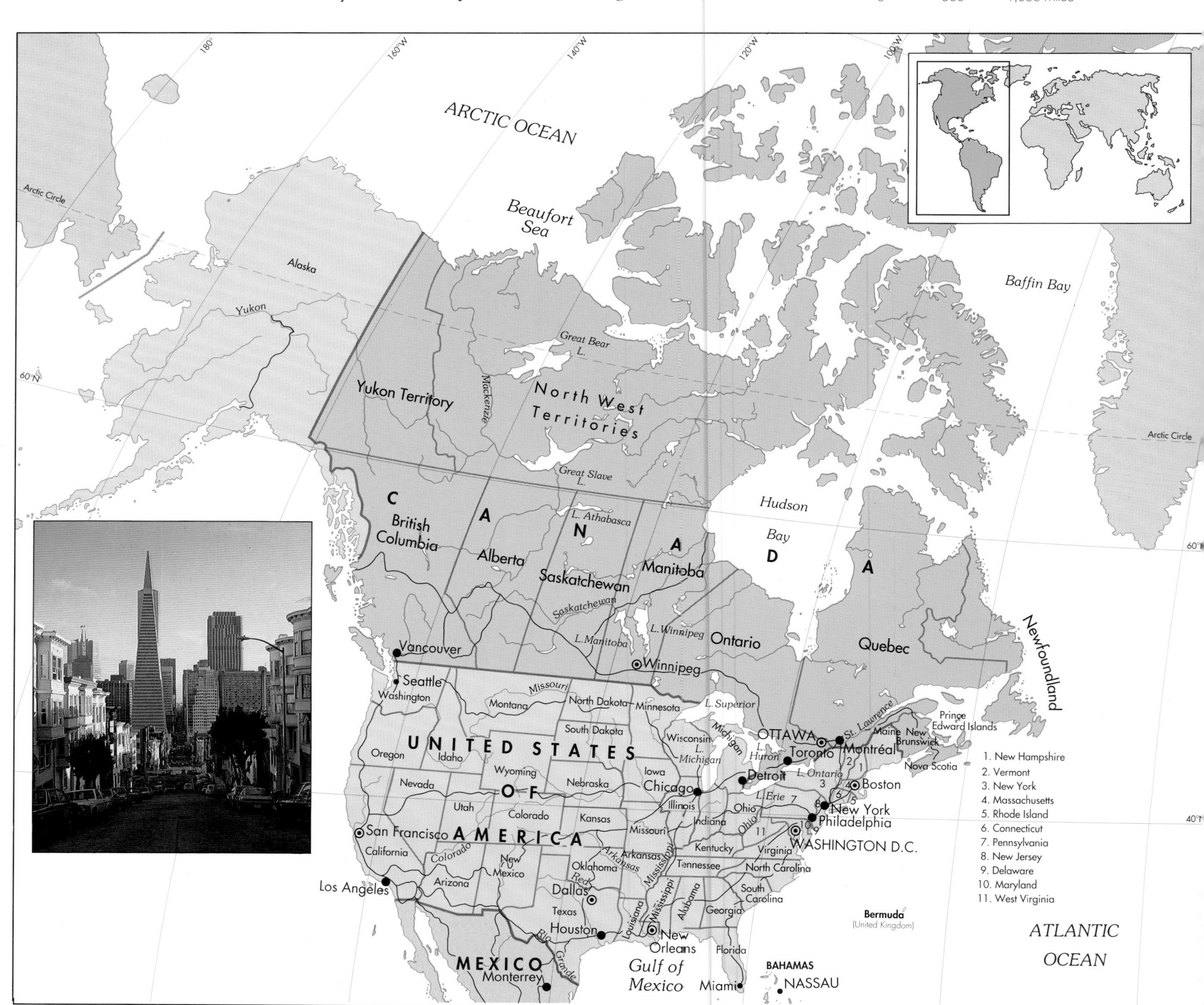

FACT CHART

- North America includes the world's second largest country (Canada) and the fourth largest (the United States). The border between the two is the longest in the world (almost 3,990 miles).
- Only the Panama Canal, opened to shipping in 1914, divides North and South America.
- The San Andreas Fault, one of the world's most active earthquake zones, runs through California.
- The Gulf of Mexico is noted for its terrible hurricanes, whirling storms which often devastate the area.
- Chile's Atacama Desert is said to be the driest place on Earth. The wettest place is probably Tutunendo, in Colombia, with an average rainfall of 456 inches each year.

The Mexican Desert
In the deserts of Mexico, the saguaro cactus and prickly pear survive by storing water in their stems. Their sharp spines prevent them from being eaten.

The Caribbean
Blue seas, white sands, and palm trees attract tourists from all over the world to Caribbean islands such as St. Lucia (see above).

Spanish Influence
Córdoba in Argentina shares its name and its style of architecture with Córdoba in Spain. The influence of colonists can be seen in local architecture throughout the Americas (see above).

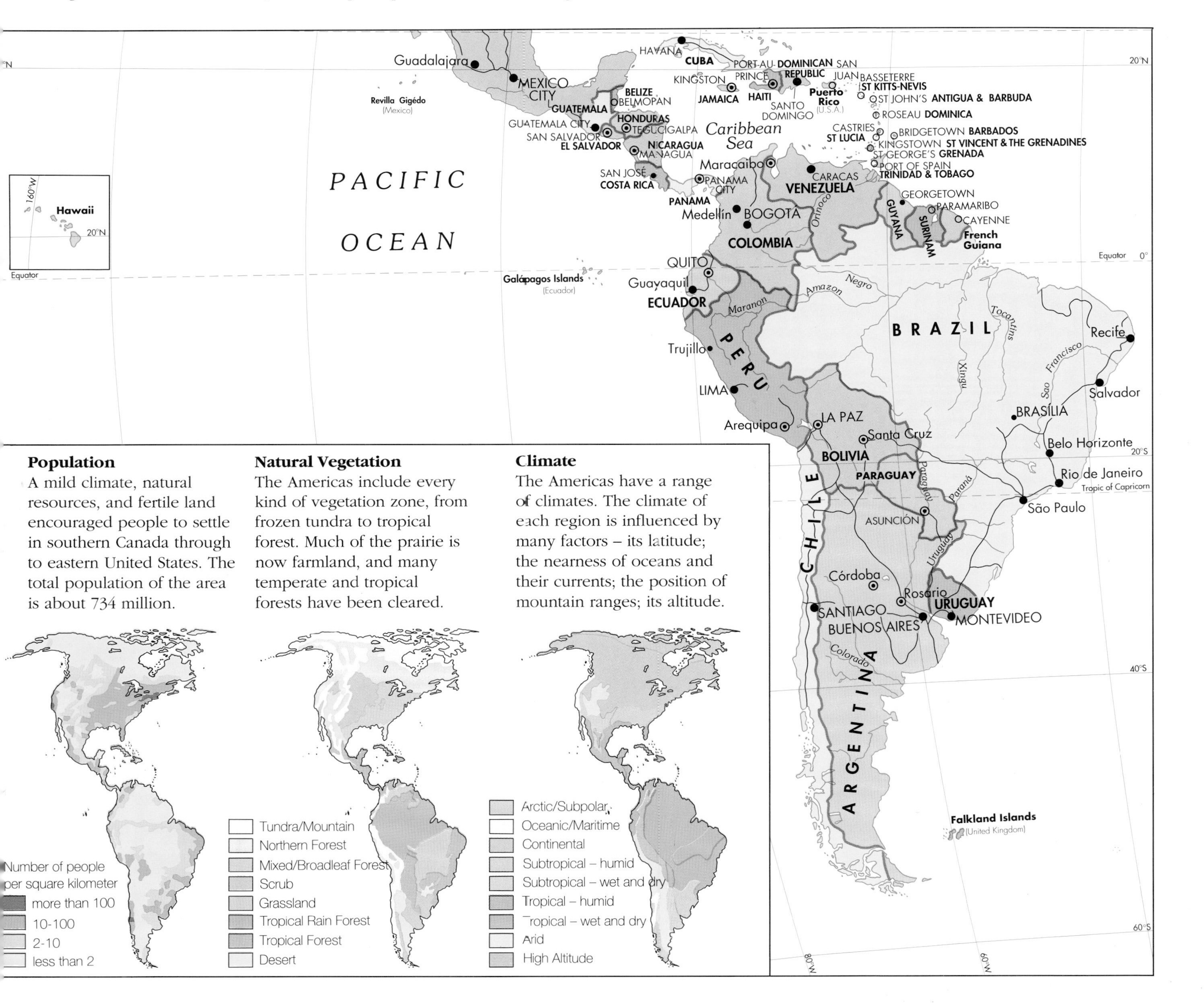

Population
A mild climate, natural resources, and fertile land encouraged people to settle in southern Canada through to eastern United States. The total population of the area is about 734 million.

Natural Vegetation
The Americas include every kind of vegetation zone, from frozen tundra to tropical forest. Much of the prairie is now farmland, and many temperate and tropical forests have been cleared.

Climate
The Americas have a range of climates. The climate of each region is influenced by many factors – its latitude; the nearness of oceans and their currents; the position of mountain ranges; its altitude.

CANADA

Canada's far north is an Arctic wilderness, with vast areas of frozen tundra and pine forests, icy mountains and lonely lakes. Most Canadians live in the south of the country, which has a milder climate. The large cities of the southeast include Toronto, Ottawa, Québec, and Montréal.

The mid-western provinces of Canada are mainly vast prairies used to raise cattle and wheat. Sawmills and lumber camps provide work in the west. Most of the sawmills are sited on the large rivers in the area. Vancouver is Canada's chief port on the Pacific coast.

Lodgepole Pine
The lodgepole (see above) grows on the slopes of the Canadian Rockies. Its long trunk was used by North American Indians as a support pole for their lodges, or teepees.

French Canada
The imposing Château Frontenac (see above) is not in France but in Québec. It was built by the Canadian Pacific Railway. The French founded Québec in 1608 and it is still French-speaking.

Toronto
Although Ottawa is Canada's capital, Toronto (see above) is its largest city, with $3^1/_2$ million inhabitants. A center of business and industry, it has many modern buildings.

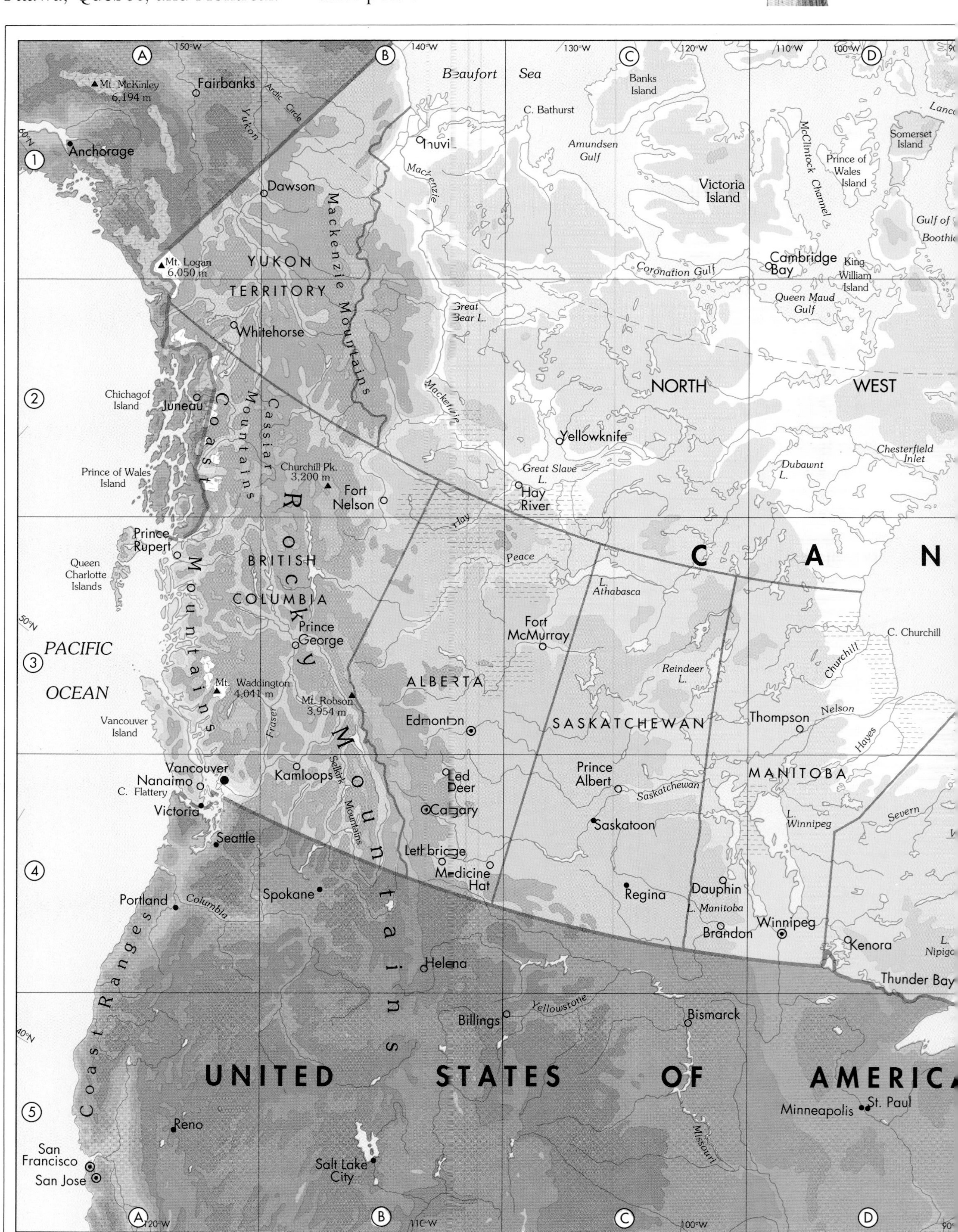

Native Americans

A traditional totem pole of carved wood (see left), painted and decorated with animals, watches over an Indian village on Canada's Pacific coast. The first people to live in Canada and the US were American Indians. Although Native Americans are now out numbered by 100 to one, many of them maintain their traditions with pride.

Animals of the Forest

Much of the coniferous forests of central Canada are still unspoilt. Animals such as moose, deer, bears, and wolves (see left) roam in them.

A Visitor's Paradise

Money from tourism is vital to Canada's economy. One of the top ten countries for holidays, people enjoy Canada's scenery (see below) and outdoor sports.

The Inuit

Inuits, meaning "the People", now live in modern cabins rather than their traditional tents of caribou skin (see above). However, some Inuit still build traditional igloos from snow blocks (see below) when on hunting expeditions.

FACT CHART

- Canada is made up of 10 provinces and two territories. The least populated regions are Yukon and Northwest Territories. The most crowded provinces are Ontario and Québec.
- The highest mountain in Canada is Mount Logan in Yukon (19,524 feet).
- The longest river in Canada is the Mackenzie (2,630 miles).
- Canada has over one million lakes – more than the rest of the world combined.
- The largest lake entirely in Canada is the Great Bear Lake (12,270 square miles).
- Canada is rich in oil and natural gas. The Trans-Canada gas pipeline is the world's longest (over 6,590 miles).
- Canada's national game is ice hockey, which was probably first played in 1855 at Kingston, Ontario.
- The Royal Canadian Mounted Police, founded in 1873, is one of the world's most famous forces. It was said that the daring "Mounties" always got their man.
- Canada has many mineral resources including copper, zinc, nickel, iron ore, gold, and lead.

Scale approximately 1:15,789,000
At the scale of this map the straight line distance from Vancouver (A4) to Quebec (F4) is approximately 2,361 miles (3,802 km).

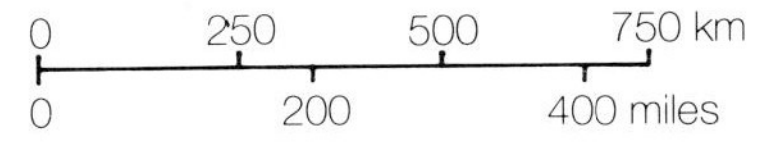

UNITED STATES OF AMERICA

The United States of America, one of the richest countries in the world, is so vast from west to east that it spans four different time zones. It is rich in natural resources with huge deposits of raw materials including oil, coal, natural gas, iron, and copper.

The fertile Great Plains that lie between the Rockies in the west and the Appalachians in the east make American farmers world leaders in agricultural produce. They export huge quantities of maize, citrus fruits, meat, milk, and wheat – one-fifth the value of all exports.

The Bald Eagle
The national symbol of the United States, the bald eagle, is now an endangered species and protected in many areas.

The Island State
Hawaii, the last state to join the Union in 1959, is made up of 130 islands in the Pacific Ocean 2,083 miles west of California. The palm-fringed beaches and tropical climate makes Hawaii a favorite holiday resort.

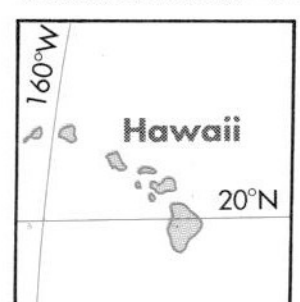

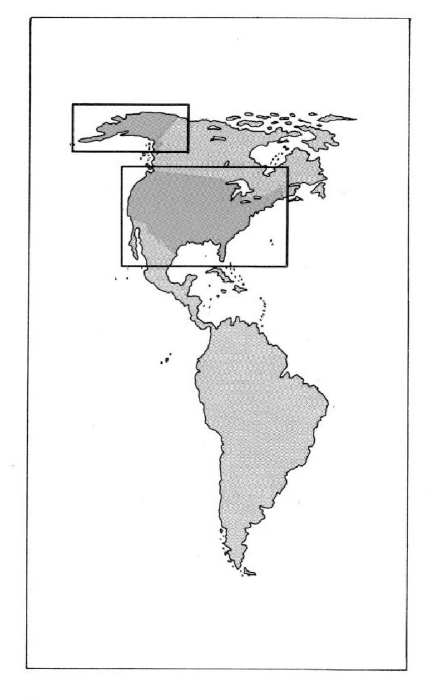

Scale approximately 1:48,550,000 (for Hawaii map only)

Scale approximately 1:12,000,000
At the scale of this map the straight line distance from Seattle (A1) to New York (H2) is approximately 2,407 miles (3,876 km).

0 200 400 500 km
0 100 200 300 miles

The Grand Canyon
Large rivers flowing across the Colorado Plateau in the southwest United States have carved huge canyons into the rock. These canyons are famous for their fantastic shapes and colors.

The Grand Canyon (see left) is over 250 miles long and between .12 and 18 miles wide; at points it towers 4,875 feet above the Colorado River.

The White House
The White House, a large mansion in Washington (see right), is the official home and office of the President of the United States.

New York City
The historic city of New York is world famous for its Manhattan skyline of towering skyscrapers (see below), especially the Empire State Building.

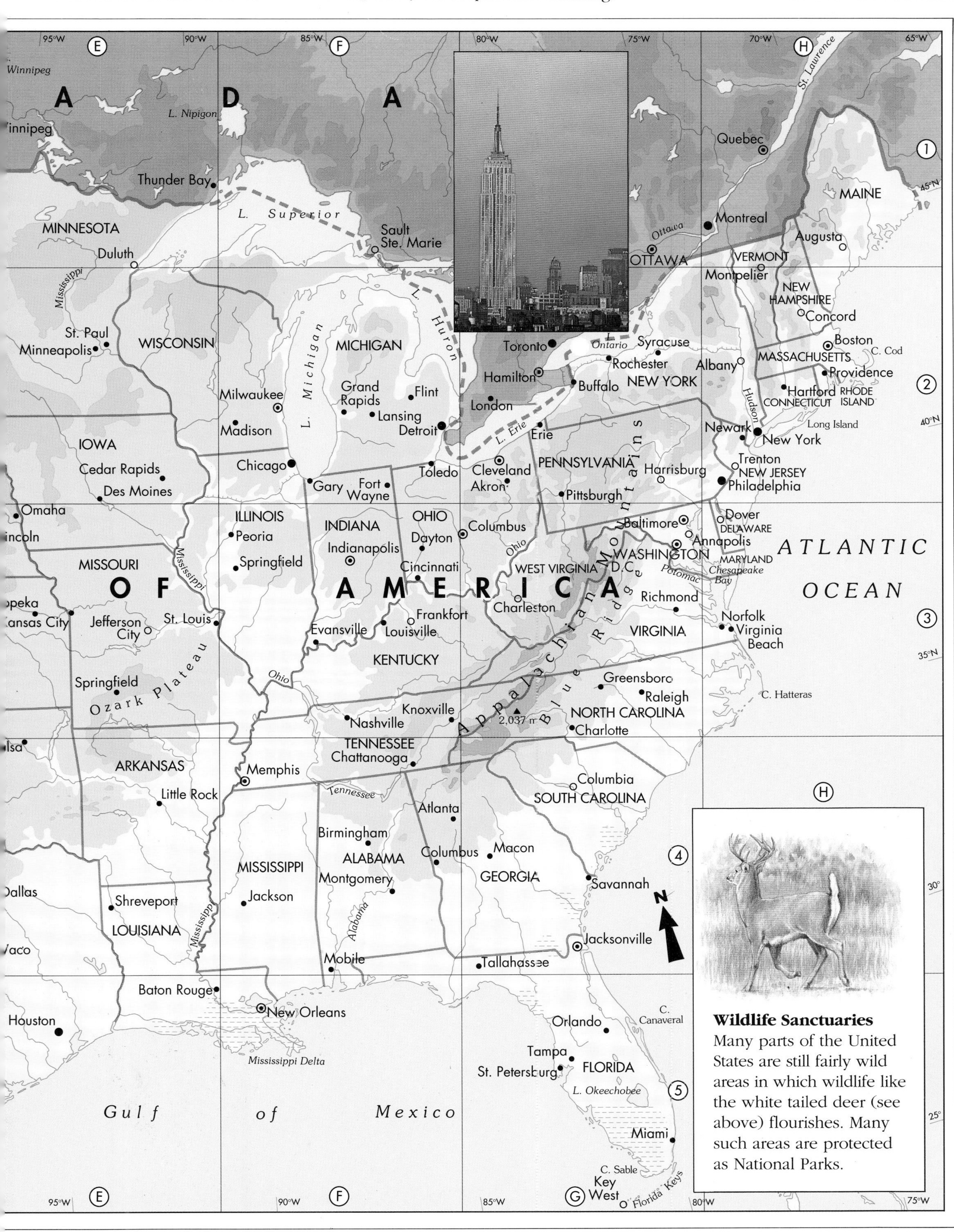

Wildlife Sanctuaries
Many parts of the United States are still fairly wild areas in which wildlife like the white tailed deer (see above) flourishes. Many such areas are protected as National Parks.

FACT CHART

- The fourth largest country in the world, the United States has almost 4.5 million miles of roads – nearly a third of a million miles are major highways and freeways.
- The Mississippi River, the longest river in North America, plus its main tributaries, the Missouri and the Ohio, drain all or part of 31 states and two Canadian provinces.
- There are 50 states, each with its own capital. The seven largest in population are California, New York, Texas, Florida, Pennsylvania, Illinois, and Ohio.
- The Stars and Stripes: the red stands for courage, the blue for justice and the white for liberty. The thirteen stripes represent the original colonies and the 50 stars the present day states.

- The national capital, Washington, lies in a specially created area – the District of Columbia – so that it is not allied to any one state.

The World's Oldest Trees
Some giant sequoias (see above) are 3,000 to 4,000 years old – the world's largest and oldest living things.

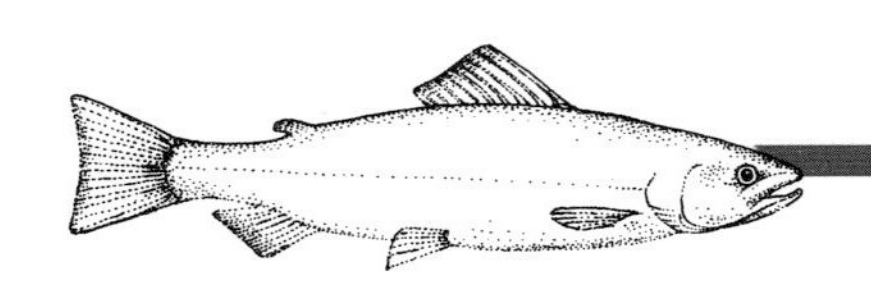

Lake Fishing
Fish of the Great Lakes include various species of cisco, the bloater, kiyi, and Atlantic salmon (see above). Overfishing and pollution have reduced the number of fish in the lakes. Some species are now extinct.

Wildlife
At sites such as Isle Royale, a US National Park in Lake Superior, one can still see the original wildlife of the Great Lakes region – moose, timber wolves, beavers (once trapped for their fur), foxes (see above), and squirrels.

Montréal
The chief city of the St. Lawrence is Montréal (see above), the largest in French-speaking Canada. Timber, paper, and grain are shipped from its river port.

Scale approximately 1:5,714,000
At the scale of this map the straight line distance from Duluth (A1) to New York (F4) is approximately 996 miles (1,603 km).

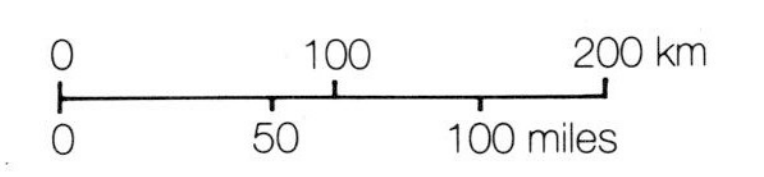

The map of North America is marked by five huge lakes. The largest is Lake Superior, in the west. In the center lie Lakes Michigan and Huron, with Lakes Erie and Ontario to the east. The US and Canadian border runs across the center of Lakes Erie, Ontario, Huron, and Superior.

The Great Lakes are bordered in many places by rocky shores, weathered cliffs, and forests of pine, birch, and sugar maple. In other parts they are bordered by highways and city skylines, for the Great Lakes region is a center of industry and the site of many great cities.

The lakes are important for commerce as they are used to ship goods from one area to another. Many locks and canals have been built so that ships can sail from Lake Superior to the oceans. The first canals were built along the St. Lawrence River as early as 1779.

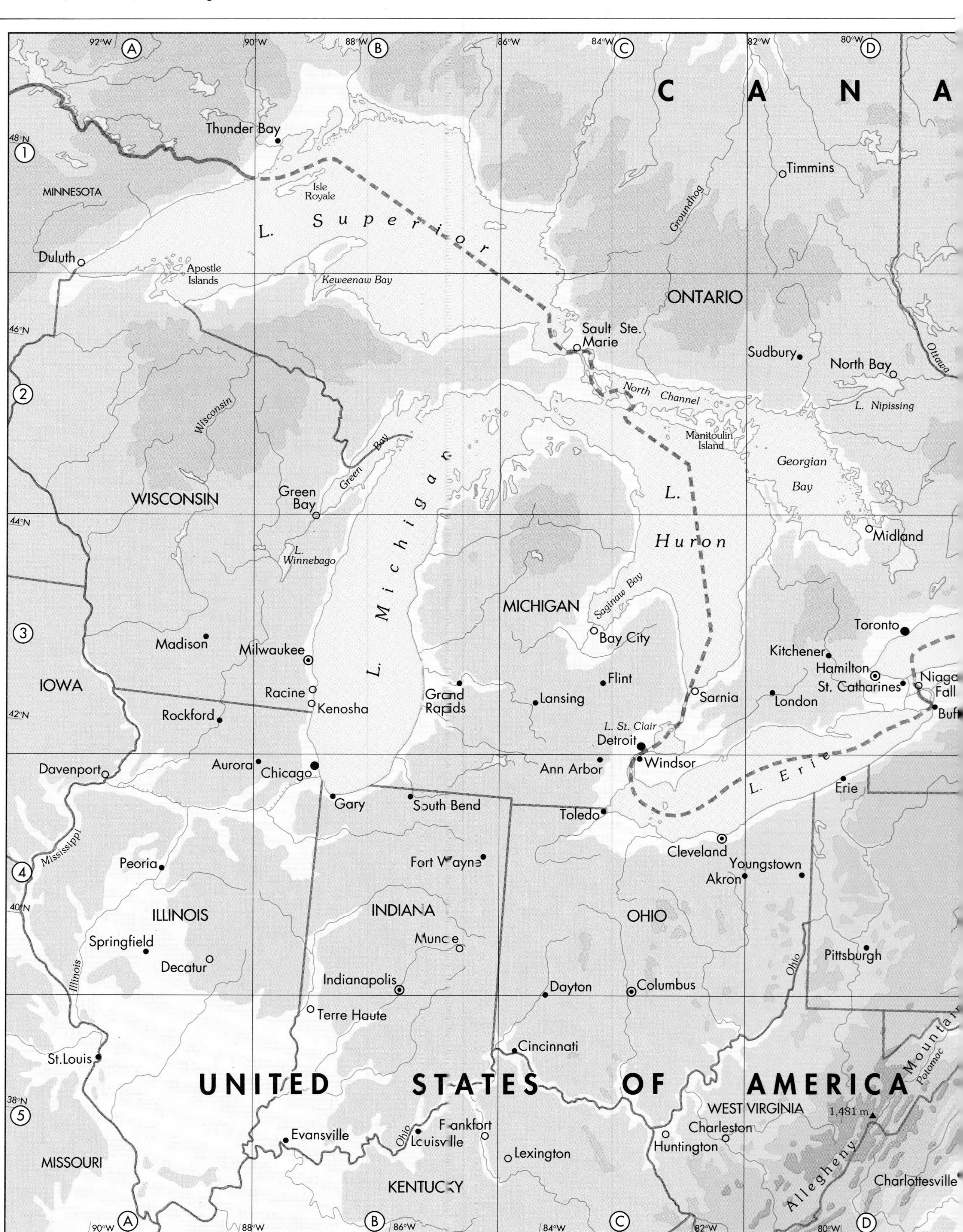

Niagara Falls
The Niagara River flows from Lake Erie into Lake Ontario. Between the two lakes it drops over two chasms. The American Falls is 1,040 feet wide and 182 feet high. The Horseshoe Falls in Canada is 2,194 feet wide and 175 feet high, a torrent of spray and foam. Both countries have built hydro-electric power stations next to the falls.

The St. Lawrence Seaway
The Great Lakes are linked to the Atlantic Ocean by the St. Lawrence River, which flows 744 miles from Lake Ontario to the sea. In the 1950s the river was widened and dangerous rapids were bypassed. This new seaway allowed sea-going vessels into the Great Lakes.

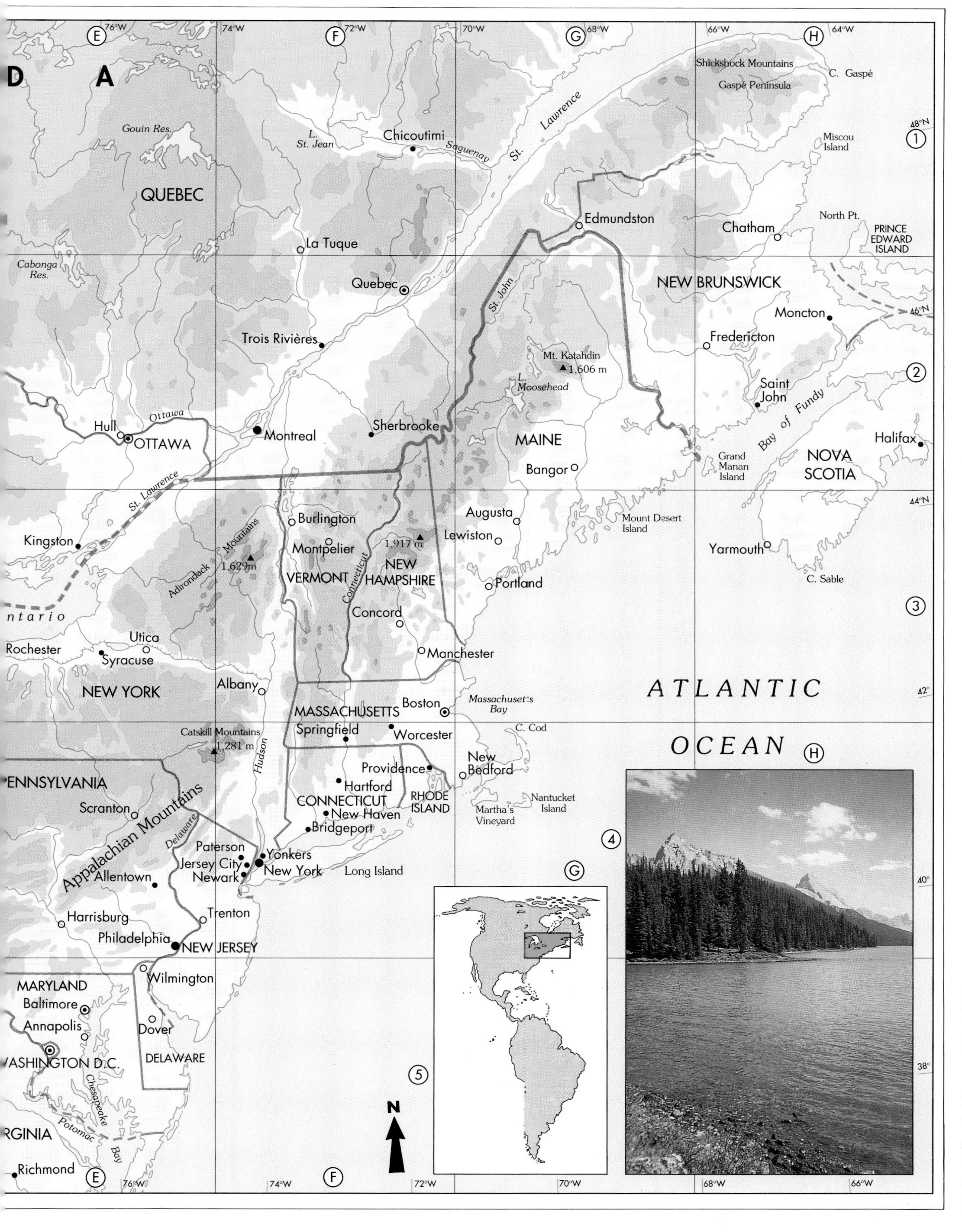

FACT CHART

- Lake Superior (31,780 square miles) covers a greater area than any other freshwater lake in the world.
- Chicago, on the western shore of Lake Michigan, is the second largest city in the United States. It boasts the world's highest skyscraper, the 1,440 feet-high Sears Tower.
- The Niagara flows at over 196,000 cubic feet per second. This immense power is now used to drive hydroelectric turbines.
- In 1859 a French showman known as Charles Blondin first crossed the Niagara Falls on a tight-rope. He later carried out the same feat blindfolded, with a wheelbarrow, and with a man on his back!
- The Great Lakes were formed long ago, after the Ice Ages. Glaciers, extending from the northern ice cap, dragged out giant scoops of rock from the face of the continent.

Industrial Heartland
The Great Lakes region is the main industrial center of Canada, with huge ports and cities. However, many areas (see left) are totally unspoilt.

CENTRAL AMERICA and THE CARIBBEAN

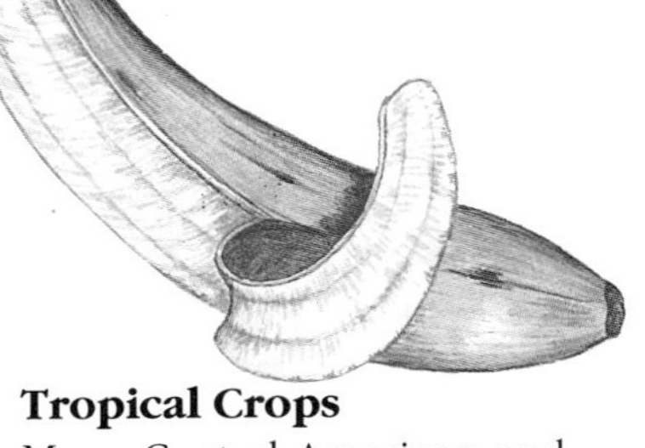

Tropical Crops
Many Central American and Caribbean countries rely on crops such as bananas, sugar cane, and coffee.

The North American continent curves and narrows to the south. Mexico is the largest country in the region. North Mexico has deserts and a high plateau between two mountain ranges. To the south lie the small countries of Central America – Guatemala, Belize, El Salvador, Honduras, Nicaragua, Costa Rica, and Panama.

To the east are the long island chains of the Caribbean Sea – the Bahamas, and the Greater and Lesser Antilles.

Cuban Fishermen
Cuba is the largest Caribbean island. Fishing provides an important export.

Hurricane Damage
Tropical storms can gust at nearly 200 miles an hour in the Caribbean, ripping up trees and houses in their path (see above).

Strange Homes
Nesting holes made by the galia woodpecker in a saguaro cactus of Mexican and Central American deserts are taken over by tiny elf owls (see above).

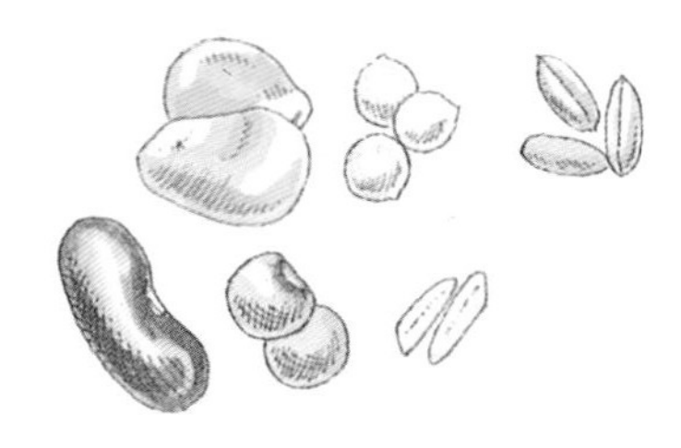

A Staple Food
Beans of many kinds are one of the main food crops of Mexico. Beans are served with chilis and *tortillas* (cornmeal pancakes).

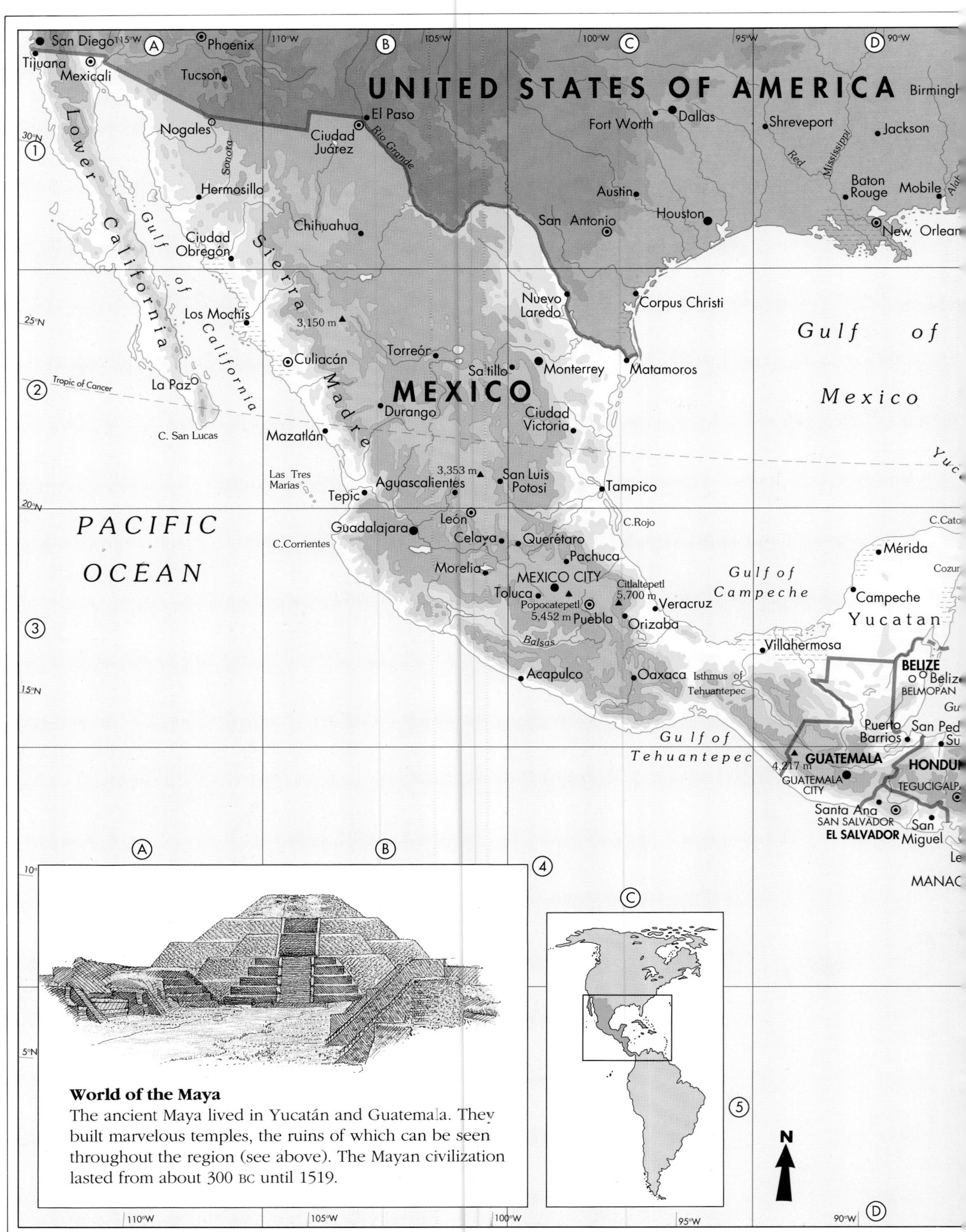

World of the Maya
The ancient Maya lived in Yucatán and Guatemala. They built marvelous temples, the ruins of which can be seen throughout the region (see above). The Mayan civilization lasted from about 300 BC until 1519.

Caribbean Homes
Many Caribbean people are poor, and their homes in the villages (see left) are often simple wooden shacks with tin roofs.

Capital of Belize
In 1961 a hurricane devastated the coast of Belize. It was decided to rebuild a modern capital, Belmopan (see right), 50 miles inland.

Endangered Turtles
Rare marine turtles such as the leatherback, the green (see above), and the hawksbill breed on the beaches of Costa Rica.

The Bahamas
The beautiful islands of the Bahamas with their waterfront markets (see left), are popular with tourists.

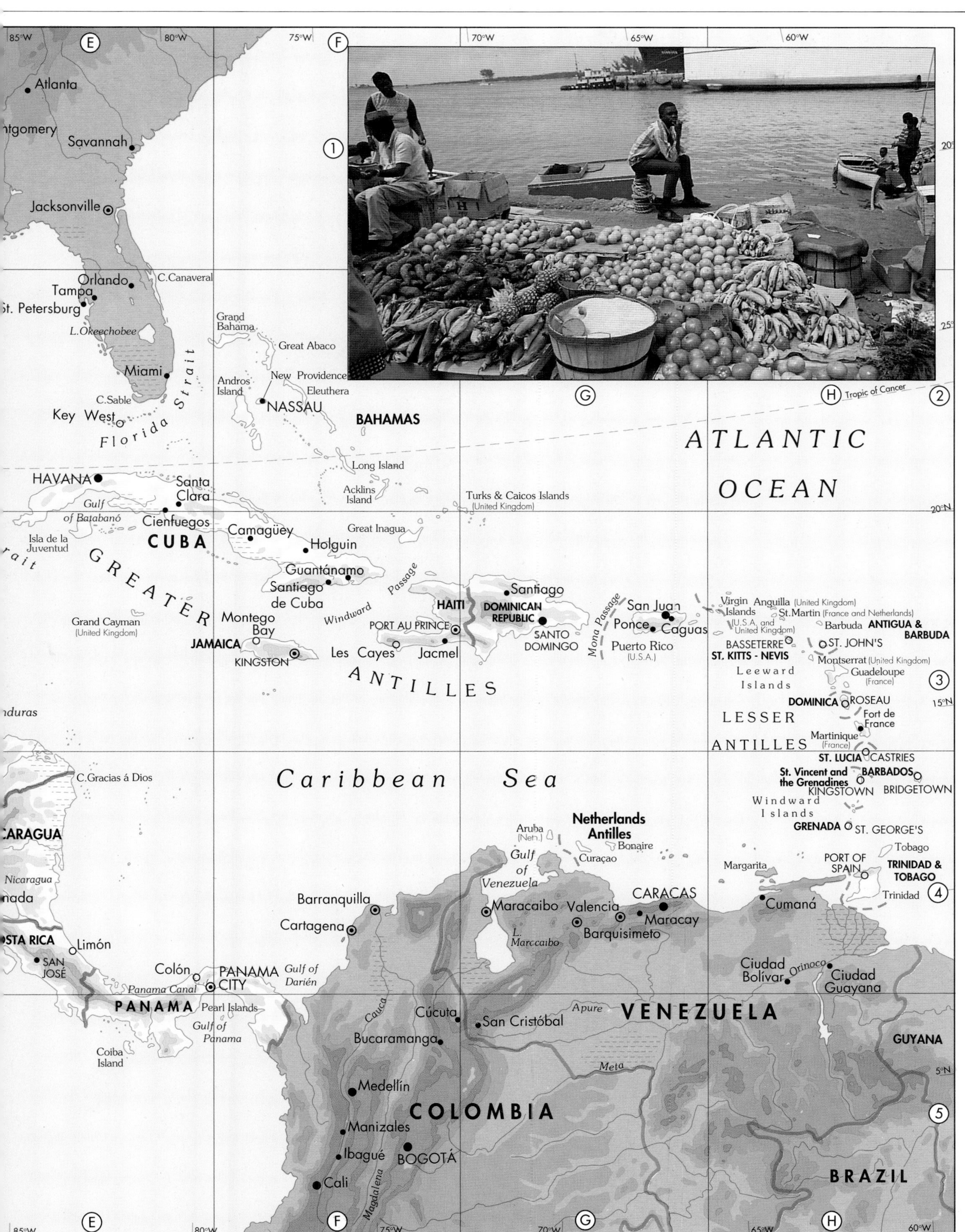

FACT CHART

- Citlaltepetl (18,697 feet), the highest peak in Mexico, is always covered in snow.
- Mexico City, one of the most crowded cities in the world, will probably have a population of over 24 million by the year 2000.
- Guatemala is the most populated Central American country with 9 million people. Belize is the least populated with 193,000.
- The Bahamas consist of 3,000 coral islands of which only 20 are inhabited.
- Tajumulco, a volcano in Guatemala, is the highest point in Central America (13,810 feet).
- The Panama Canal was completed in 1914. It is used as a short cut between the Pacific and Atlantic Oceans.

Antigua
Antigua, in the Lesser Antilles, with its sandy beaches and blue sea is a haven for holidaymakers.

Scale approximately 1:15,000,000
At the scale of this map the straight line distance from Guatemala City (D4) to Bridgetown (H4) is approximately 2,075 miles (3,342 km).

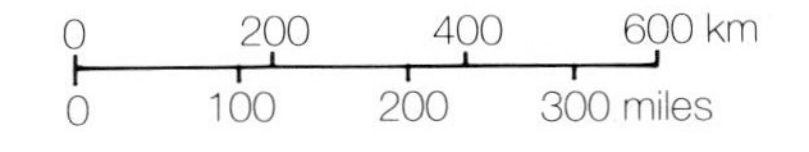

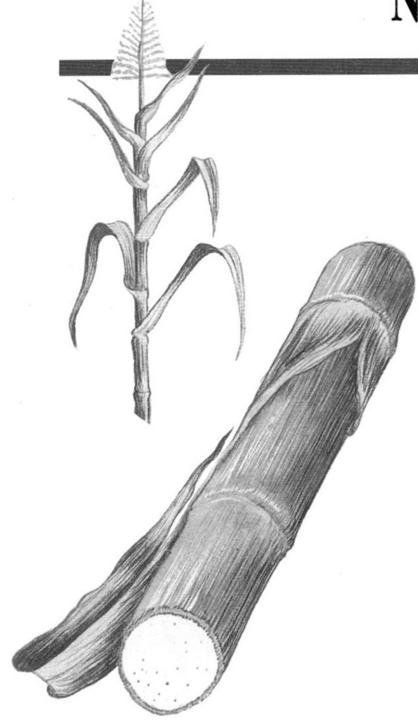

Sugar Cane
The tropical climate of Guyana makes it ideal for growing sugar cane and there are large plantations. One region, Demerara, has given its name to a kind of brown sugar.

The Andes mountain range, which dominates Ecuador in northwest South America, continues into Colombia and Venezuela. To the east and west of the Andes lie dense rain forests which extend northwards from the Amazon basin. The flat coastal regions of Venezuela take in the vast, swampy delta of the Orinoco.

The landscape varies from the coastal strip of Guyana, where sea walls, dykes, and canals help to keep the water out, to the forested mountains of Surinam. Much of the interior of French Guiana is a wilderness.

FACT CHART

- The light wood from balsa trees of the jungles of Ecuador was once used to make ocean-going rafts.
- Colombia's longest river is the Magdalena (965 miles).
- Over 80 percent of Surinam is covered by mountainous rain forest.
- The world's highest waterfall lies on a branch of the River Carrao in Venezuela. The Cherun-Meru, known in English as the Angel Falls, has a total height of 3,212 feet.
- Cotopaxi (19,344 feet) in Ecuador is the world's highest active volcano.
- Lake Maracaibo in Venezuela, one of the first areas to be developed for offshore oil production, is the largest in the region (5,150 square miles).
- The Andes are the longest mountain chain in the world – 4,500 miles.
- Devil's Island in French Guiana housed the world's most notorious prison until it was closed in 1945.

Scale approximately 1:10,127,000
At the scale of this map the straight line distance from Quito (B4) to Paramaribo (G2) is approximately 1,663 miles (2,678 km).

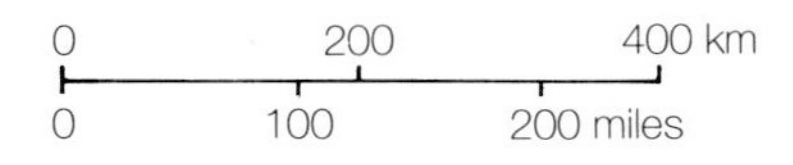

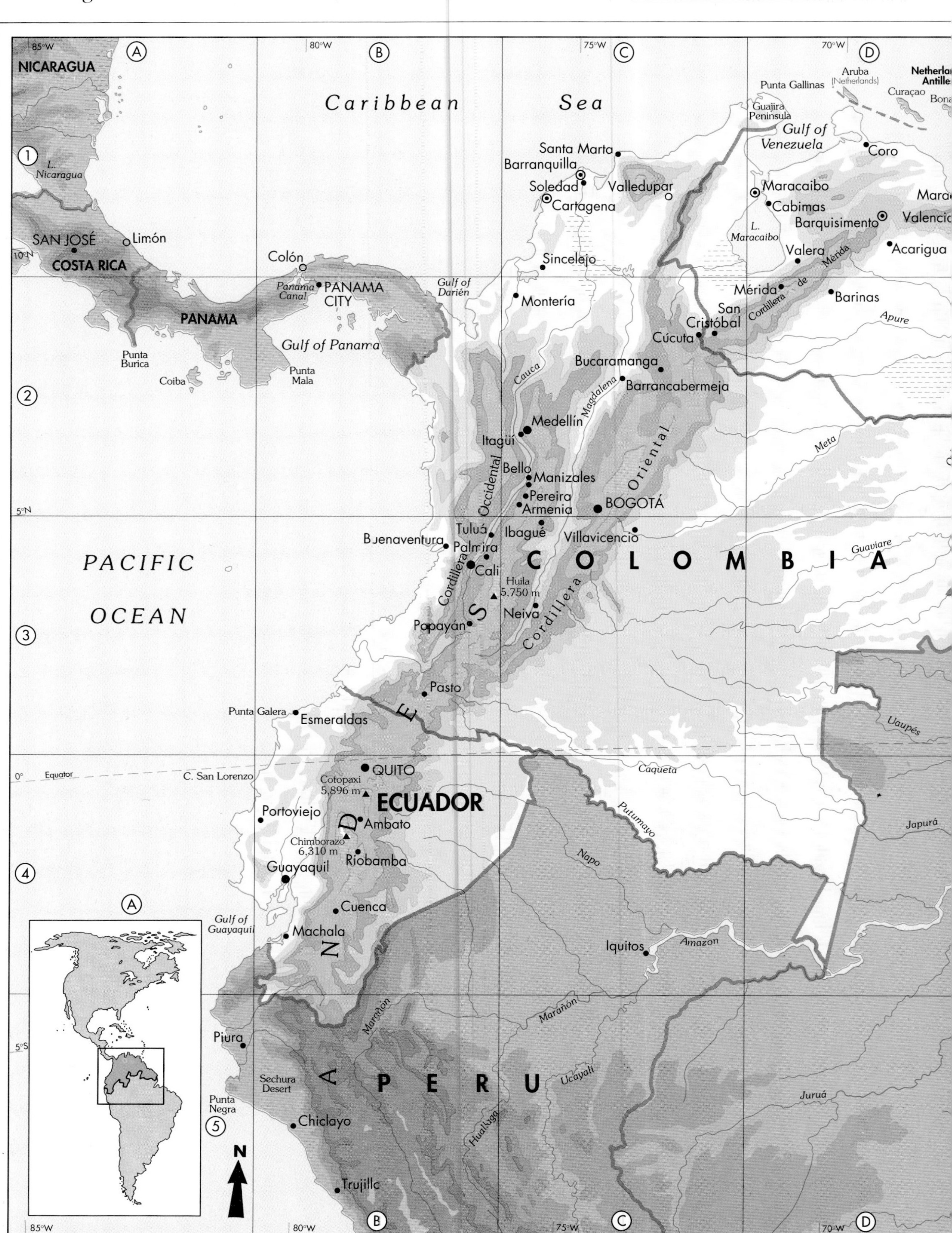

Ecuador

Ecuador takes its name from the Equator, on which it lies. Most of the people live in the valleys. Cattle and sheep are raised and sold at market. This is often the women's job (see left).

Mining in French Guiana

Bauxite, the ore used to make aluminum, is mined in French Guiana, which has many mineral deposits.

Wildlife in Danger

Rain forest covers the interior of the region. It is a treasure house of animal species, including parrots and monkeys (see right and below). Many species are threatened by forest clearance for roads, farmland, and mining. River creatures, too, are in danger, including the boto, a river dolphin, and the black caiman.

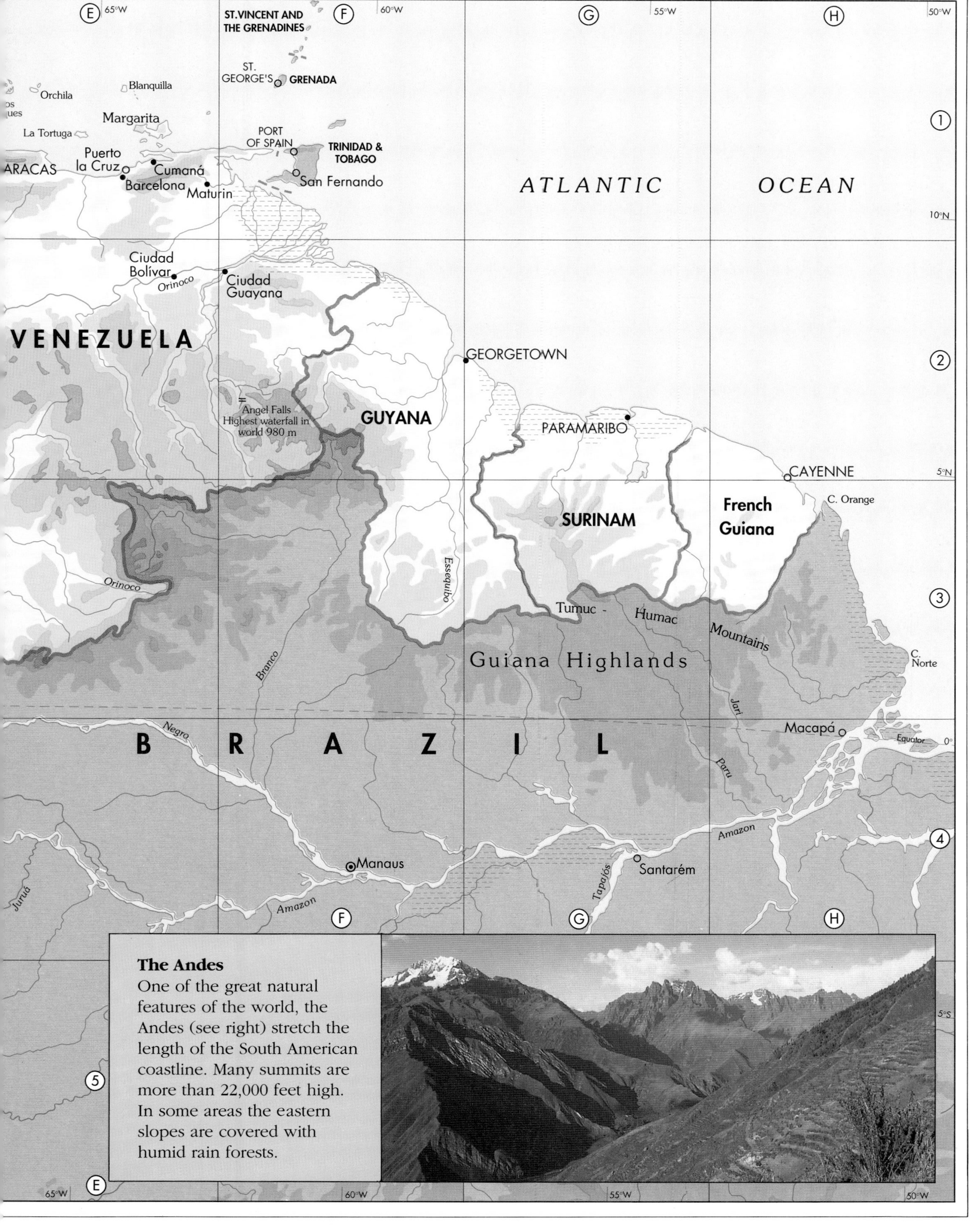

The Andes

One of the great natural features of the world, the Andes (see right) stretch the length of the South American coastline. Many summits are more than 22,000 feet high. In some areas the eastern slopes are covered with humid rain forests.

Wealth from Oil

Venezuela has rich reserves of oil. Production is centered on the Maracaibo region. Further oil fields lie beneath the Orinoco basin and offshore below the Caribbean Sea. Large oil refineries (see below) attract many workers.

SOUTHERN SOUTH AMERICA

The high mountain chain of the Andes runs southwards through Peru, Bolivia, and Chile. Chile is 2,666 miles long but only 93–124 miles wide. The continent's largest country is Brazil, which takes in the vast Amazon basin, the highlands of the southeast, and the coastal cities. Paraguay and Uruguay are lands of fertile hills and plains, given over to farming. Argentina's grasslands, the *pampas*, are grazed by large herds of cattle. Further south lie the remote plateaus of the Patagonia region and the bleak wilderness of Tierra del Fuego.

Antarctic Beech
This tree braves the cold winds of the southern Andes and the remote islands of southern Chile. It can reach a height of 90 feet in more sheltered areas. It often grows alongside lenga and monkey-puzzle trees.

FACT CHART

- The Amazon is the second longest river in the world – 4,000 miles from the Peruvian Andes to the South Atlantic. The forests are home to many Amazon Indian tribes.

- The Andes were home to many great civilizations, such as that of the Incas. Their empire, based around Cuzco, in Peru, flourished from 1300 until the Spanish invasion of 1532.
- Lake Titicaca in Bolivia and Peru is the largest lake in the region (3,220 square miles) and the highest navigable lake in the world.
- Mount Aconcagua in Argentina and Chile is the highest peak in the region (22,830 feet).
- Parts of the Atacama Desert in Chile have not had rain for over 400 years – it is the driest place on Earth.

Scale approximately 1:20,000,000
At the scale of this map the straight line distance from Belém (E1) to Montevideo (D5) is approximately 2,352 miles (3,787 km).

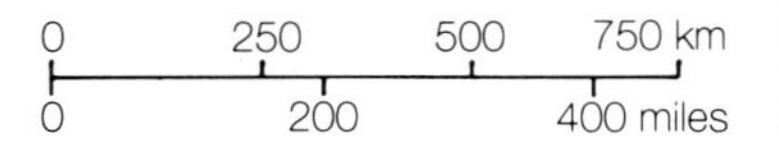

Brazilian Cowboys
Brazil, like Argentina, has large herds of beef and dairy cattle. These herds are tended by teams of cowboys on horses.

Buenos Aires
The capital of Argentina (see right), Buenos Aires lies on the banks of the Rio de la Plata. It was once the main port of Argentina.

Palm Huts
Throughout South America, shacks of palm leaves (see above) and wood or tin exist alongside modern skyscrapers of concrete and steel.

The Brazilian Forest
The Amazon rain forest is the largest in the world. Its clearance threatens wildlife (see above), plants, and the Indian tribes who live there.

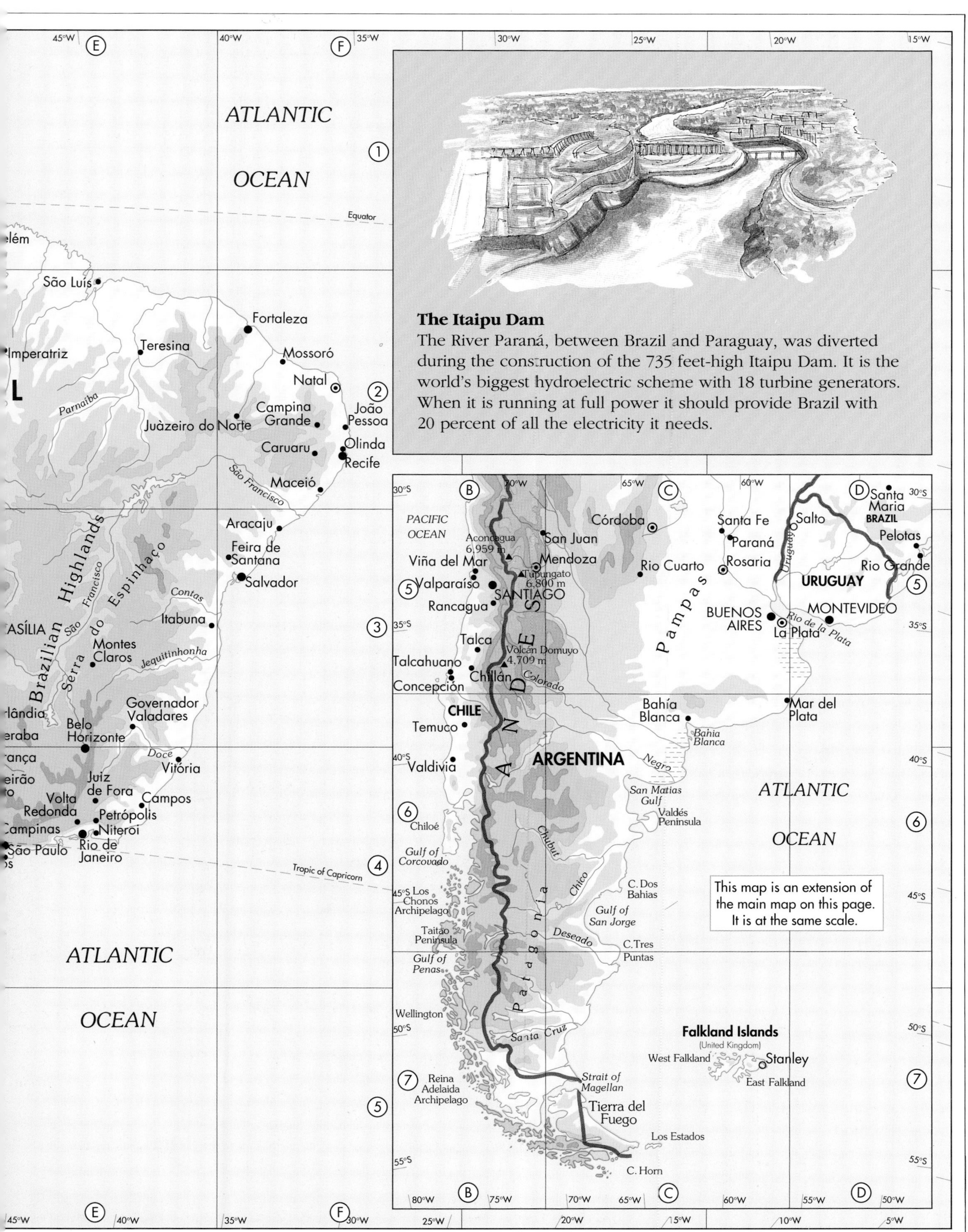

The Itaipu Dam
The River Paraná, between Brazil and Paraguay, was diverted during the construction of the 735 feet-high Itaipu Dam. It is the world's biggest hydroelectric scheme with 18 turbine generators. When it is running at full power it should provide Brazil with 20 percent of all the electricity it needs.

Patagonian Oil
Oil and natural gas are produced at the port of Comodoro Rivadavia. There are further plans to develop industry in this remote region.

A Varied Wildlife
The region is famous for its amazing wildlife such as the peccary (a piglike animal) and the armadillo from Argentina (see above).

ARCTIC OCEAN

Animal Life
Polar bears (see below), which live on the Arctic tundra and ice floes are expert hunters. Their main food, seals (see above), live in the water and crawl out onto the ice to sunbathe.

FACT CHART

- At the North Pole, the sun does not rise above the horizon for six months of the year and it is dark all the time. For the other half of the year the sun never sets.
- The Arctic contains valuable minerals, including coal, oil, copper, nickel, iron, and gold.
- Sea temperatures average 32°F in July and –40°F in January.
- The first man to reach the North Pole was an American, Robert Peary. He traveled over the ice with teams of dogs in 1909.
- In 1958 the US nuclear-powered submarine *Nautilus* crossed the Arctic Ocean under the ice, passing the North Pole on the way.

Baffin Island
Baffin Island (see right) is a high plateau with mountains, glaciers, and snowfields rising to 8,000 feet. Part of it is protected as the Anyuittuq National Park.

Scale approximately 1:26,650,000
At the scale of this map the straight line distance from the North Pole (C2) to Jan Mayen (D4) is approximately 2,365 miles (3,806 km).

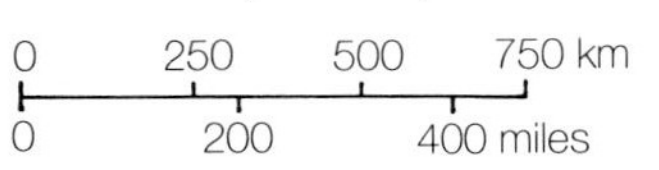

The Arctic, the smallest of the world's major oceans, is 3,300 miles across, with the North Pole at the center. Most of the ocean is covered in ice. In some parts there are patchy ice floes 5 feet thick, with clear water between them. In other parts, the solid masses of ice are over 50 feet thick.

The Arctic is only about 17,850 feet at its deepest part. Areas of continental shelf project out from the surrounding landmasses. These are thought to contain large deposits of oil and minerals.

Right Whale
Whales have been hunted so much that their numbers have severely diminished. The Greenland and black right whale (see above) are slow-moving and easily captured. They are now protected species.

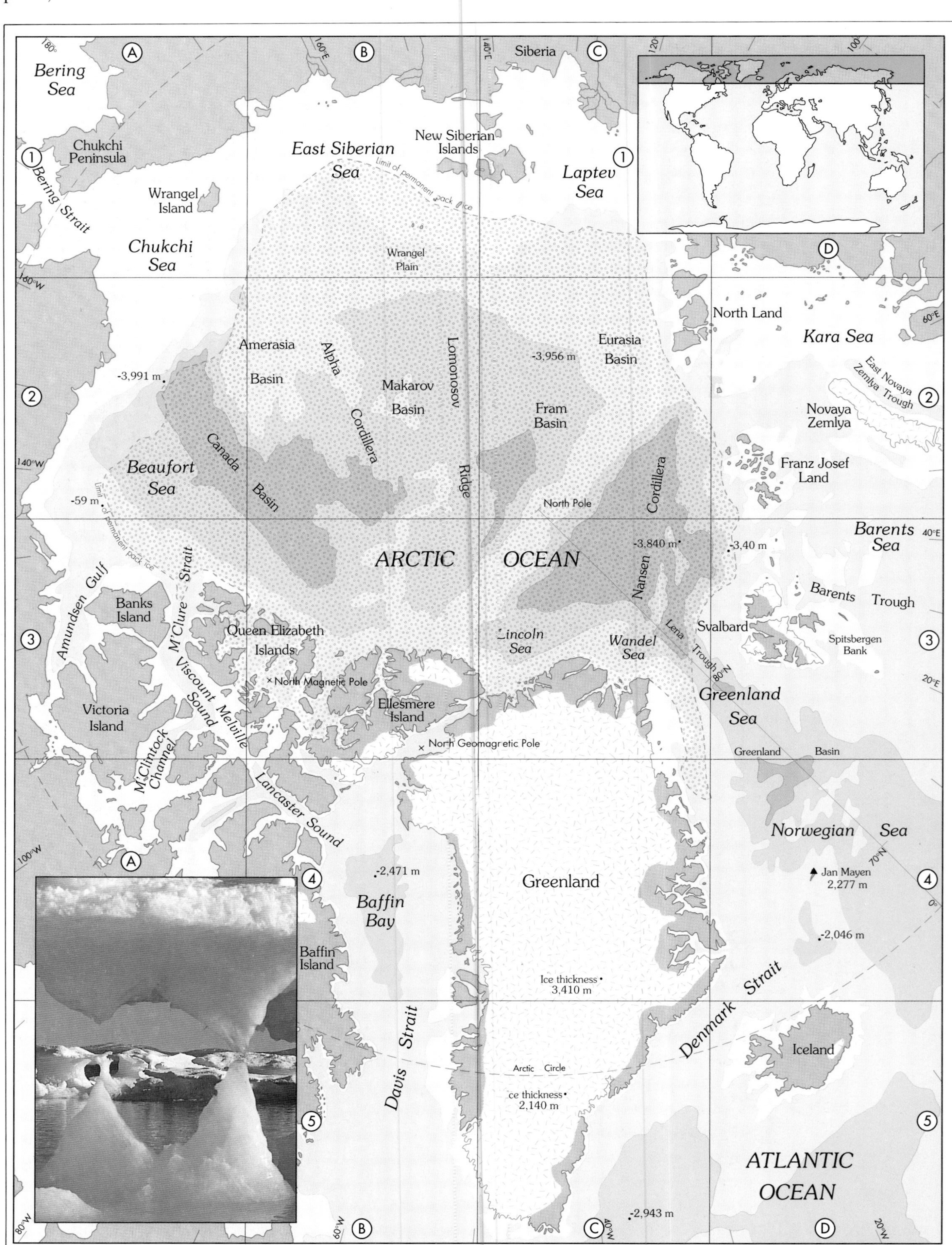

ANTARCTICA and the SOUTHERN OCEANS

Blue Whale
The blue whale (see above), the largest animal in the world, can grow to 100 feet long and weigh up to 120 tons.

A Land of Ice
A very thick ice-cap covers Antarctica (see below), forming a vast plateau that rises to 9,000 feet.

Whereas the Arctic is an ocean surrounded by land, Antarctica is a continent ringed by water. The Southern Ocean is the world's stormiest ocean. Blizzards blow north at great speeds and can last for days.

Antarctica is much colder than the Arctic. For most of the year pack-ice covers the ocean's two main arms, the Weddell and Ross Seas. In summer many icebergs are released and float north to latitude 55°S and even further. The only humans in Antarctica are visiting scientists and explorers.

Cold Water Fish
There are few plants and no land animals in the Antarctic, but the ocean teems with life, including the antifreeze fish (see above) which can survive freezing temperatures.

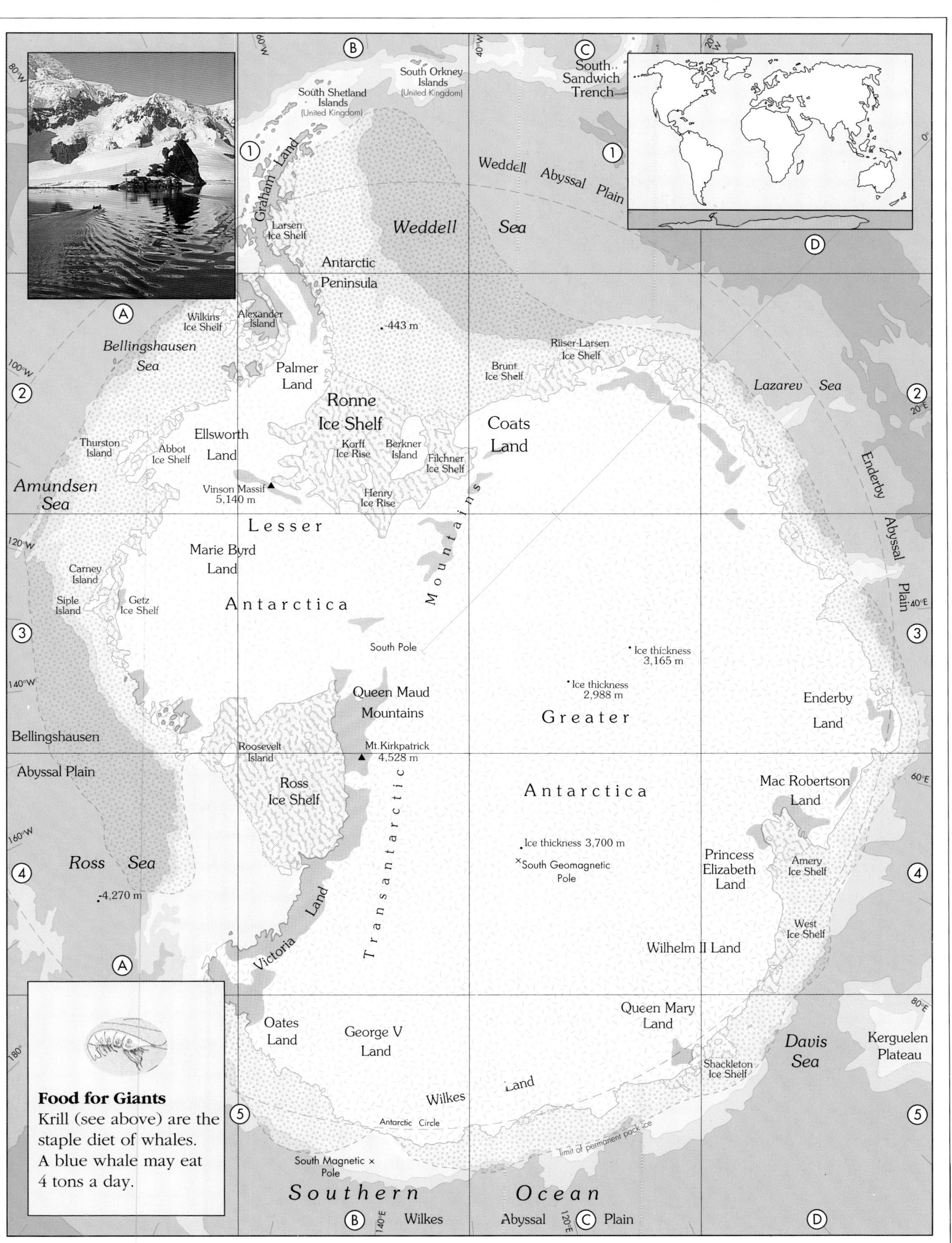

Food for Giants
Krill (see above) are the staple diet of whales. A blue whale may eat 4 tons a day.

Penguins
The emperor penguin (see above) is native to Antarctica. At 3 feet tall, it is the largest of the penguin species.

FACT CHART

- One of the biggest icebergs ever recorded in the Southern Ocean was the size of Belgium. Large bergs may drift in the ocean currents for many years, gradually being eroded into fantastic shapes.
- A record low temperature of –126°F was recorded at a research base on Antarctica.
- At the South Pole in central Antarctica the ice-cap is about 8,930 feet thick.
- The first person to reach the South Pole in 1911 was Roald Amundsen, a Norwegian. He was followed 35 days later by Captain Robert Scott leading a British expedition. Scott and his party died on the return journey.
- The Greenland glacier is the largest glacier in the Northern Hemisphere (700,000 square miles).

Scale approximately 1:22,700,000
At the scale of this map the straight line distance from the South Pole (B3) to the South Shetland Islands (B1) is approximately 2,352 miles (3,787 km).

0 500 1,000 km
0 300 600 miles

Coral Reefs
The coral reefs of the Pacific Ocean are home to all kinds of tropical fish, including the Moorish Idol (see above) and brightly colored angelfish (see below).

Floating Stings
Jellyfish (see below) have a mass of stinging tentacles. They use their stings to paralyze small fish and other prey.

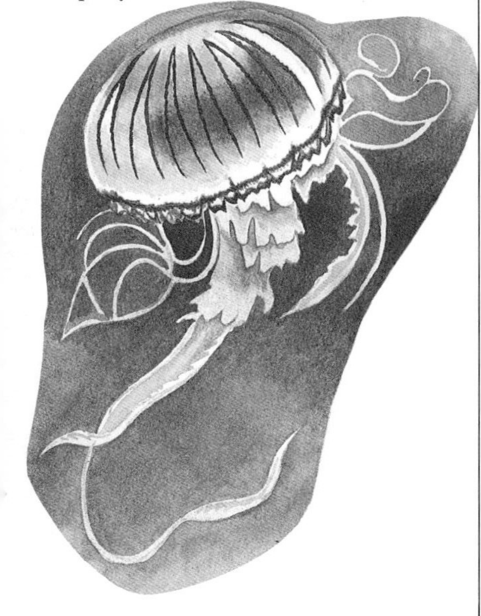

Coral Islands
Many of the Polynesian islands in the Pacific like Cook Island (see above) are surrounded by coral reefs, which are composed of the chalky remains of millions of tiny animals.

The Pacific Ocean, the world's largest expanse of sea, covers a third of its surface. It extends over several plates of the earth's crust. As a result the seabed is not smooth, but contains deep trenches, high ridges, and shallow basins. There are also thousands of islands. Many of them are volcanic mountains; their underwater peaks become covered with coral to form reefs or atolls.

The Indian Ocean is the third largest ocean in the world. A ridge shaped like an upside-down Y divides it into two parts. One arm passes around southern Africa and joins the Mid-Atlantic Ridge, while the other joins with another ridge which lies beyond Australia.

The Panama Canal
The Panama Canal is an important route for shipping. Ships can save about 8,000 nautical miles by using it instead of Cape Horn (see below).

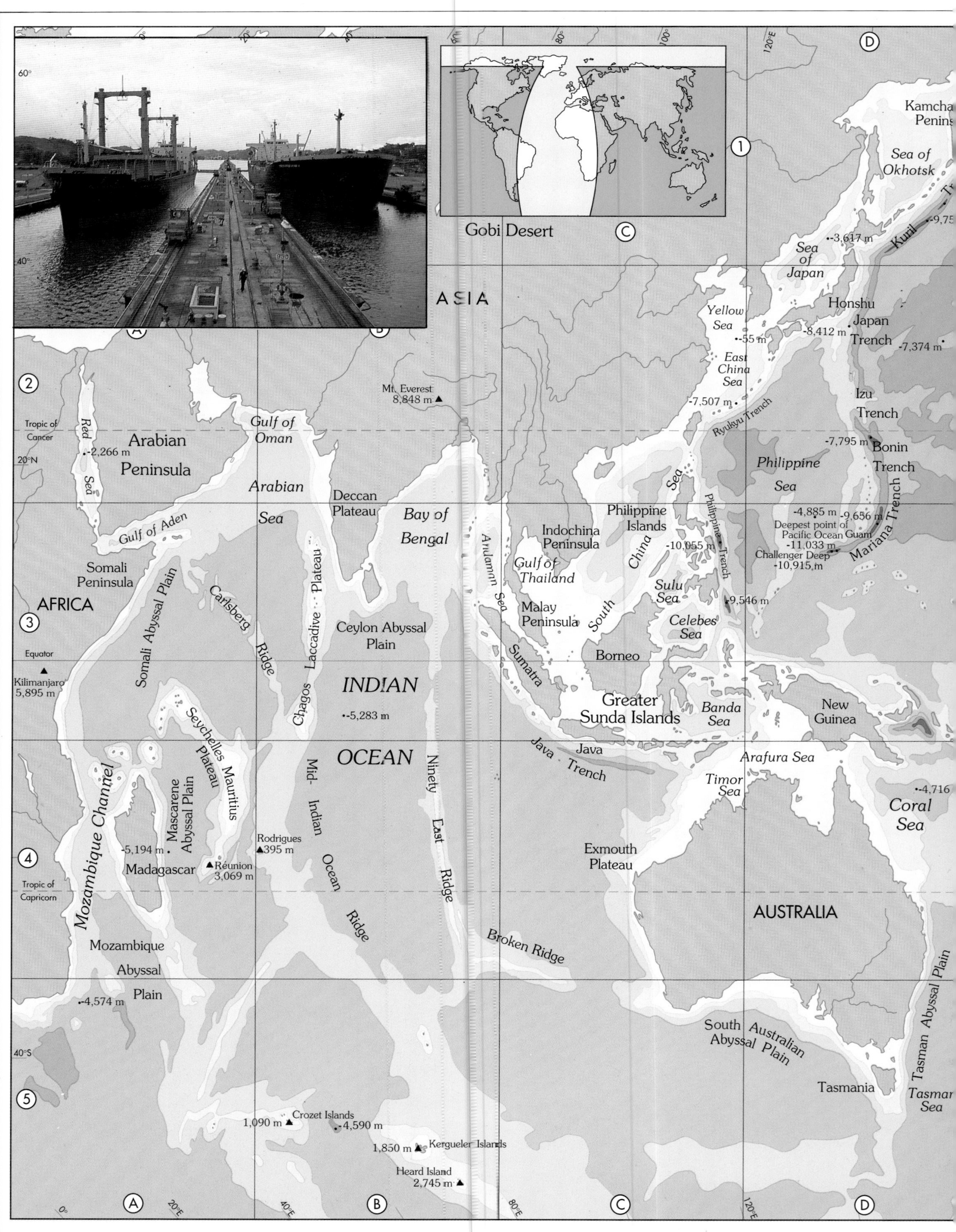

Mangrove Swamps
Mangrove forests grow along the muddy shores of tropical countries such as Malaysia. The extensive roots of the trees trap mud and silt, and this eventually builds up into new areas of land.

Sea Life
Many whales (see above) live in the Pacific and Indian Oceans. There are also many kinds of fish including sailfish and about 50 species of flying fish (see right). They all have very large pectoral fins, or "wings".

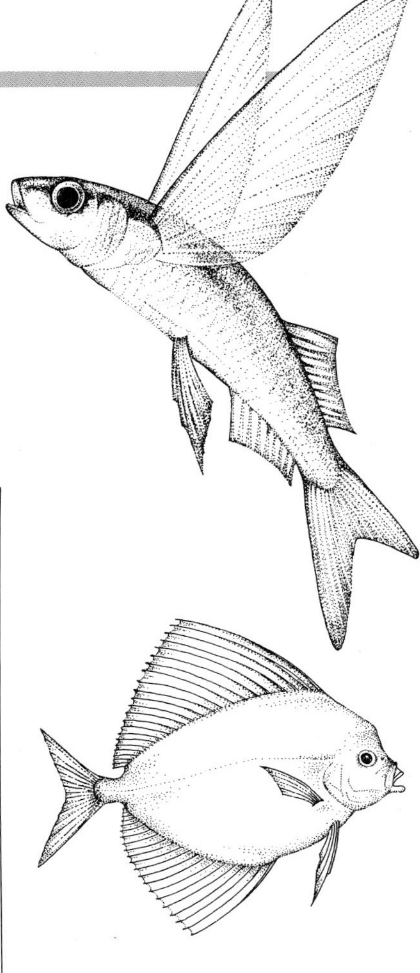

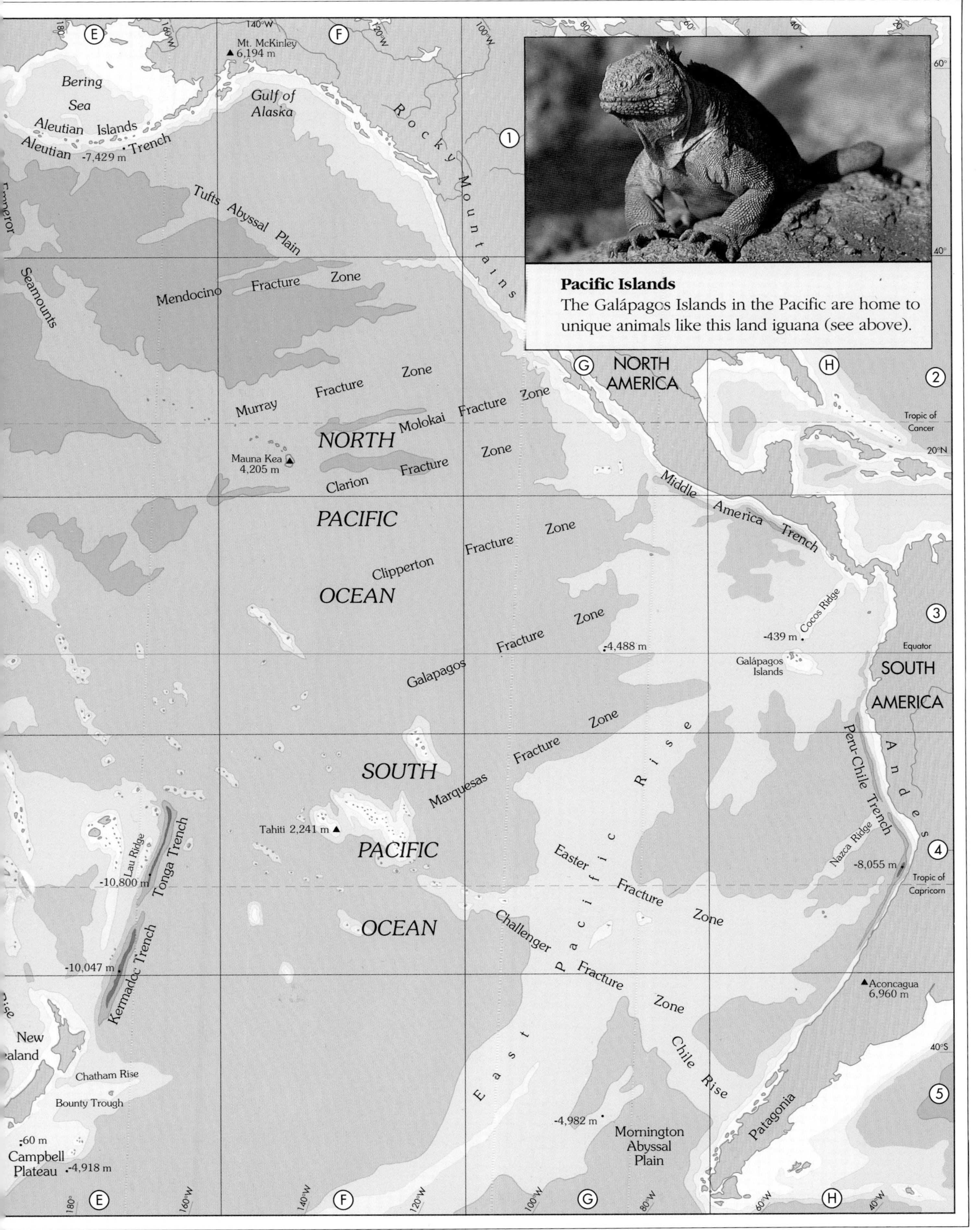

Pacific Islands
The Galápagos Islands in the Pacific are home to unique animals like this land iguana (see above).

FACT CHART

- The Marianas Trench, southwest of the island of Guam in the Pacific Ocean, is the deepest known region of the earth's surface. It is 36,198 feet below sea level – deep enough to contain Mount Everest.
- The Roaring Forties is a belt of strong westerly winds lying between 40°S and 50°S of the Equator in the Indian Ocean. There is no large landmass in the area to disrupt the airflow, and the winds are often gale force.
- The Galápagos are a group of 13 islands situated on the Equator in the Pacific Ocean. Giant tortoises, some of which are 400 years old, live on the islands. Many of the native animals and birds are found nowhere else in the world.
- Mauna Kea, a volcano on Hawaii, is 13,800 feet high. If it is measured from the sea floor and not from sea level, it is 33,474 feet high, taller than Mount Everest.
- The first European to sail across the Pacific Ocean in 1520 was the Portuguese explorer Ferdinand Magellan. He called it Pacific, meaning "peacefully," because he met with gentle and steady winds.

Scale approximately 1:60,000,000
At the scale of this map the straight line distance from Réunion (A4) to Tahiti (F4) is approximately 6,525 miles (10,500 km).

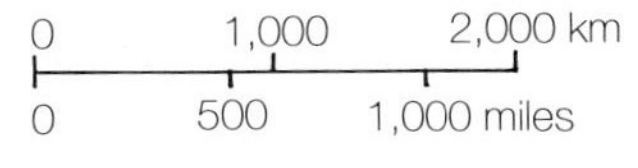

ATLANTIC OCEAN

North Sea Oil
Large reserves of natural gas and oil have been discovered beneath the North Sea (see above).

The Atlantic is the second largest ocean, and the youngest. Two hundred million years ago America was joined to Europe. Gradually, at a speed of just over an inch a year, the plates containing these countries began to separate and crack. Later, the land between these cracks slipped down to form a large valley. This gap now measures over 3,000 miles across and is filled with the Atlantic Ocean.

Mediterranean Pollution
The Mediterranean has virtually no tides. Pollution is a serious problem because there are no currents to flush away wastes (see below).

The waters of the Atlantic move in two giant circuits of currents. Some currents are warm; others are cold. The contrast in sea temperatures, together with the cold currents from the Poles, causes storms, particularly in the North Atlantic.

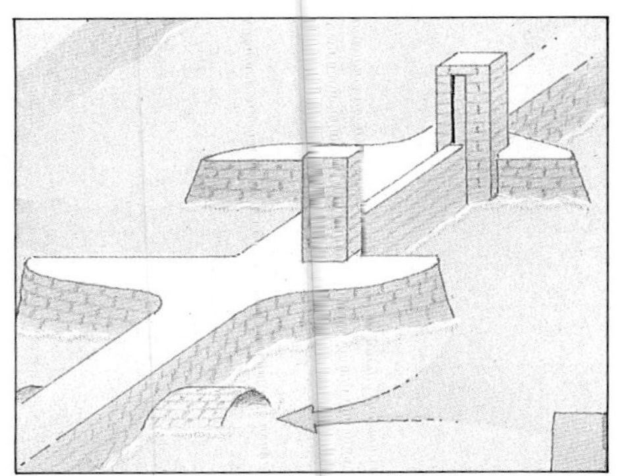

Rich Fishing
The shallow waters of the continental shelf surrounding Europe and along the coast of North America are rich fishing grounds.

Tide and Wave Power
Many countries plan to use tide and wave power to generate electricity. In pilot plants, the water flow through the barrages (see left) is used to drive electricity generators.

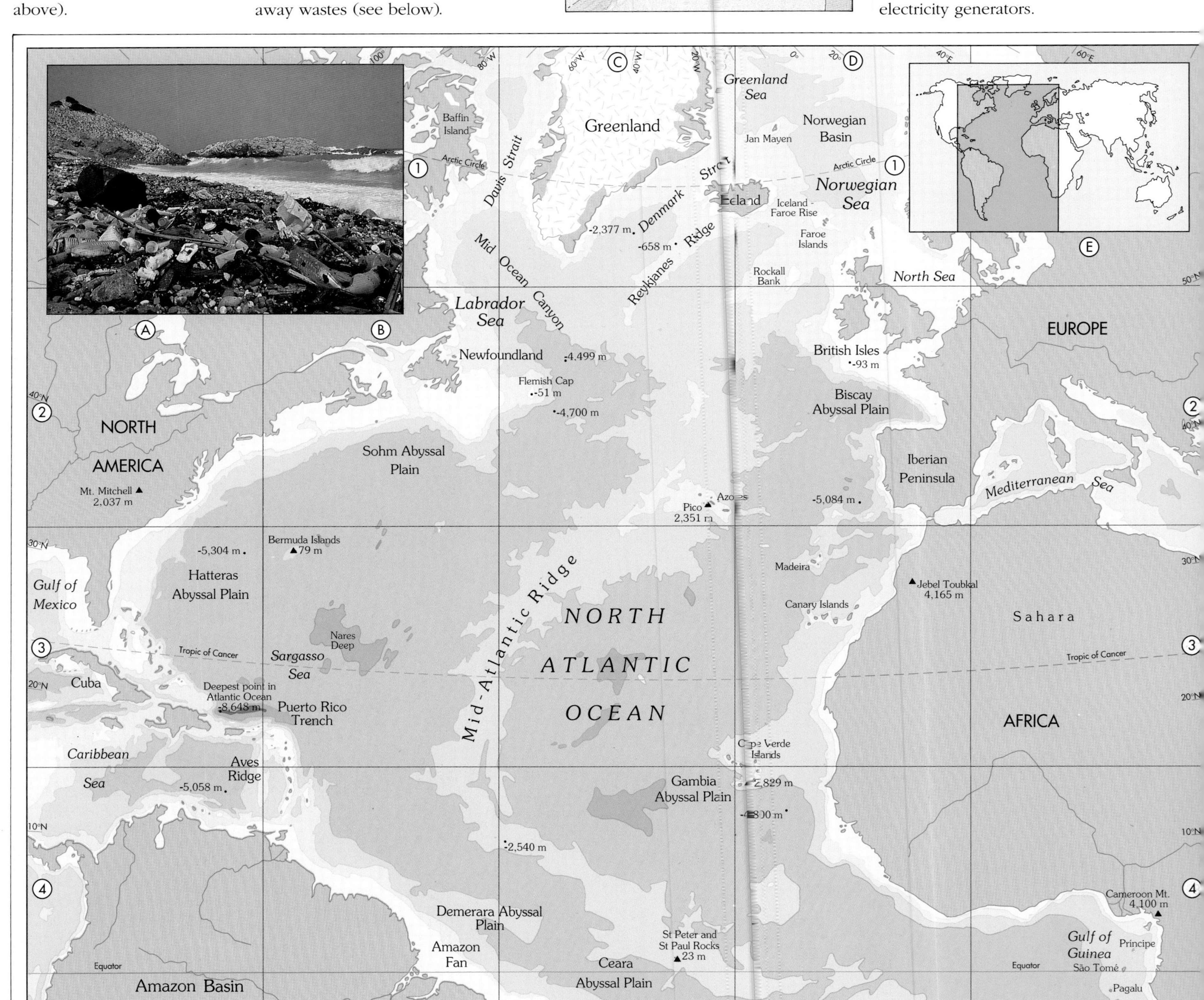

FACT CHART

- The average depth of the Atlantic is 10,925 feet.
- Because of ocean currents in the North Atlantic, places that are the same distance from the North Pole sometimes have very different temperatures. Labrador is no further north than the British Isles, but it has long, cold winters and the average temperature is well below zero.
- The Gulf Stream is a warm Atlantic current. It starts in the Caribbean, then flows into the Gulf of Mexico and through the Florida Straits. It travels northwards at 80 miles a day, bringing a temperate climate to the coastal areas in its path.
- Eels from European and North American rivers travel to the Sargasso Sea to breed. It lies at the center of the North Atlantic currents and is warm and still throughout the year.

Deep-sea Exploration
Deep-sea exploration in the Atlantic Ocean (see left) has revealed nodules made of a valuable metal called manganese. The nodules also contain other useful minerals such as copper, nickel, and aluminum. Large reserves of petroleum and gas have also been discovered, which represent about 90 percent of the Atlantic's available mineral resources.

Underwater Animals
Dolphins live in the warmer parts of the Atlantic and in the Mediterranean. Schools of these sociable animals may include up to 200 individuals. Ridley turtles, also live in the warmer seas, returning to the land to lay their eggs. Kemp's Ridley, the smallest and most endangered species, is found only in the Atlantic.

Scale approximately 1:42,105,000
At the scale of this map the straight line distance from Bermuda (B3) to Tristan da Cunha (D6) is approximately 6,142 miles (9,885 km).

0 500 1,000 1,500 km
0 300 600 900 miles

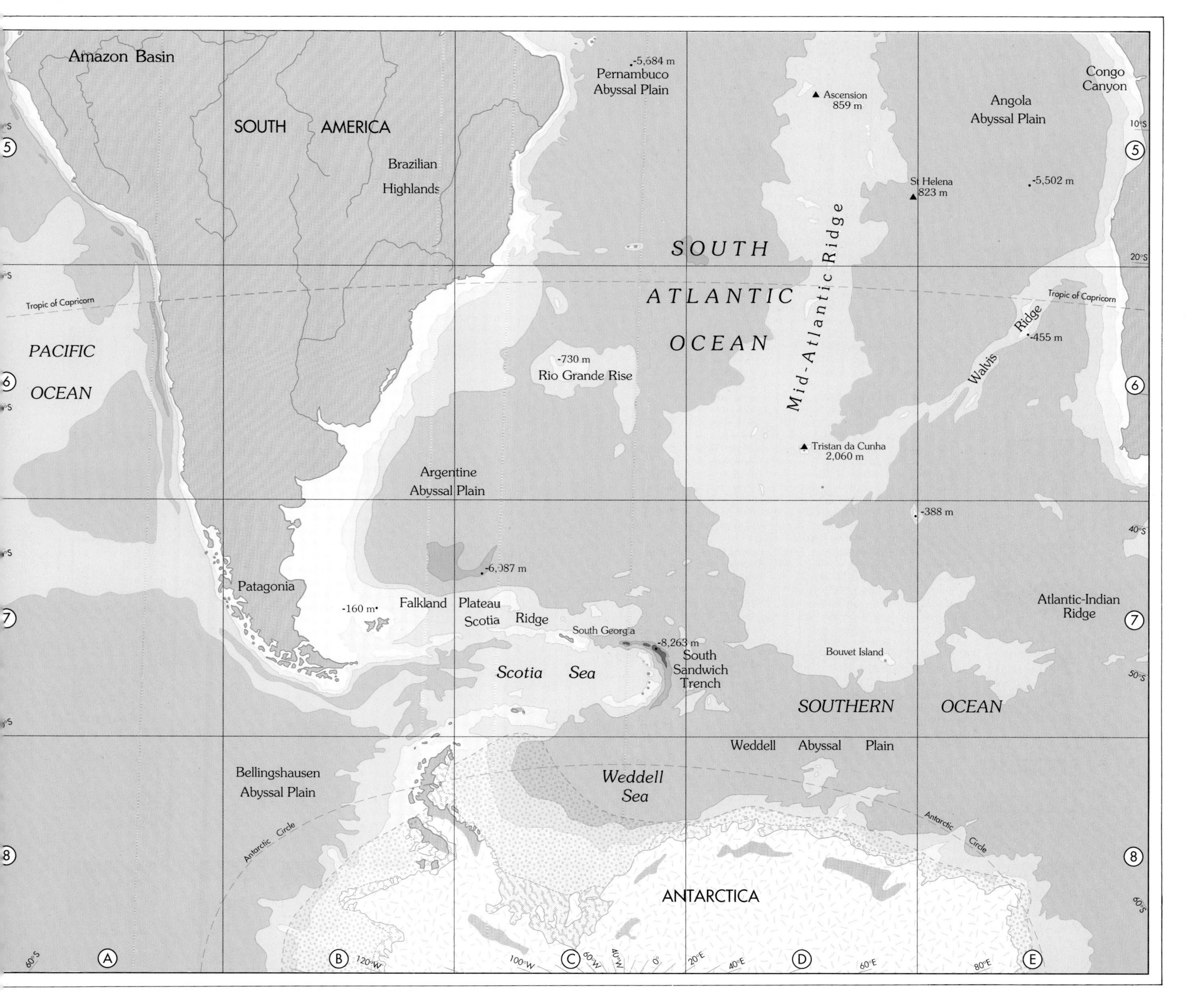

EUROPE key facts

In this section you can find some useful facts and figures about each country. The countries are listed in alphabetical order. At a glance, you can find out the population of Hungary; the area of Nepal; the capital of Kenya; the language spoken in Croatia; the religion of Mexico, or the currency used in Iceland.

The flags of each country are also pictured. These are listed in geographical order in an anti-clockwise direction.

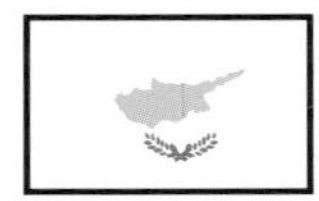
Cyprus

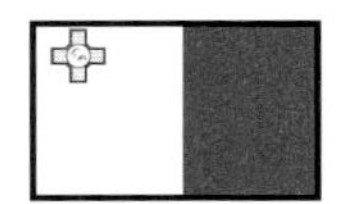
Malta

San Marino

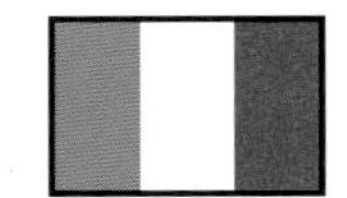
Italy

Croatia

Slovenia

Bosnia & Hercegovina

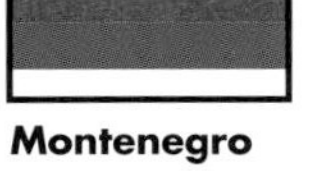
Montenegro

Iceland

Norway

Sweden

Finland

Ireland

United Kingdom

Denmark

Netherlands

Belgium

Luxembourg

State Name	Area(sq. miles)	Population	Capital	Language	Religion	Currency
Albania	11,097	3,200,000	Tirana	Albanian	Atheist until 1990	Lek
Andorra	181	51,400	Andorra-la-Vella	Catalan	Roman Catholic	Franc & Peseta
Austria	32,369	7,600,000	Vienna	German	Roman Catholic	Austrian schilling
Belgium	11,780	9,930,000	Brussels	Flemish, French	Roman Catholic	Belgian franc
Bosnia & Hercegovina	19,736	4,000,000	Sarajevo	Serbo-Croat	R.C., Orthodox, Islam	Dinar
Bulgaria	42,812	8,970,000	Sofia	Bulgarian	Orthodox	Lev
Croatia	21,824	4,600,000	Zagreb	Serbo-Croat	Orthodox, R.C.	Dinar
Cyprus	3,571	698,800	Nicosia	Greek, Turkish	Greek Orthodox, Islam	Cyprus pound
Czech Republic	30,449	10,331,200	Prague	Czech	R.C., Protestant	Koruna
Denmark	16,627	5,140,000	Copenhagen	Danish	Lutheran	Danish krone
Finland	130,708	4,970,000	Helsinki	Finnish	Lutheran	Markka
France	209,930	56,180,000	Paris	French	Roman Catholic	French franc
Germany	137,781	70,070,000	Berlin	German	Protestant, R.C.	Deutsche mark
Greece	50,935	10,140,000	Athens	Greek	Greek Orthodox	Drachma
Hungary	35,910	10,590,000	Budapest	Hungarian	R.C., Protestant	Forint
Iceland	39,758	253,500	Reykjavik	Icelandic	Lutheran	Krona
Ireland	27,129	3,540,000	Dublin	English	Roman Catholic	Irish pound
Italy	116,289	57,600,000	Rome	Italian	Roman Catholic	Italian lira
Liechtenstein	62	28,181	Vaduz	German	Roman Catholic	Swiss franc
Luxembourg	998	378,400	Luxembourg	French, German	Roman Catholic	Luxembourg franc
Macedonia*	9,928	2,100,000	Skopje	Macedonian, Albanian	E. Orthodox, Muslim	Macedonian Dinar
Malta	122	354,900	Valletta	English, Maltese	Roman Catholic	Maltese lira
Monaco	.75	29,376	Monaco	French	Roman Catholic	French franc
Montenegro*	5,333	615,267	Podgorica	Serbo-Croat	Orthodox, Muslim	Dinar
Netherlands	16,160	14,890,000	Amsterdam	Dutch	Protestant, R.C.	Guilder
Norway	125,017	4,200,000	Oslo	Norwegian	Lutheran	Norwegian krone
Poland	120,696	37,930,000	Warsaw	Polish	Roman Catholic	Zloty
Portugal	35,506	10,300,000	Lisbon	Portuguese	Roman Catholic	Escudo
Romania	91,675	23,000,000	Bucharest	Romanian	Orthodox	Leu
San Marino	23.6	22,746	San Marino	Italian	Roman Catholic	Italian lira
Serbia*	34,116	9,791,745	Belgrade	Serbo-Croat	Orthodox, Muslim	Dinar
Slovak Republic	18,932	5,300,000	Bratislava	Slovak	R.C., Protestant	Koruna
Slovenia	7,817	1,900,000	Ljubljana	Serbo-Croat	Orthodox, R.C., Isl.	Dinar
Spain	194,834	39,540,000	Madrid	Spanish	Roman Catholic	Peseta
Sweden	170,198	8,500,000	Stockholm	Swedish	Lutheran	Swedish krona
Switzerland	15,939	6,700,000	Bern	German, French	Protestant, R.C.	Swiss franc
United Kingdom	94,223	57,240,000	London	English	Protestant, R.C.	British pound

*Serbia and Montenegro are recognised by the UN as part of Yugoslavia, whereas Macedonia, formerly a part of Yugoslavia, is an independent state.

Macedonia

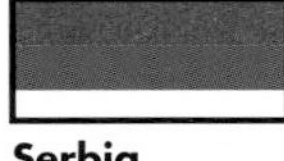
Serbia

Albania

Greece

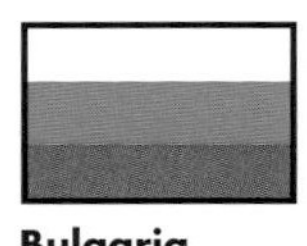
Bulgaria

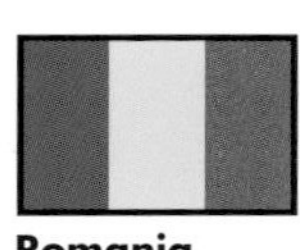
Romania

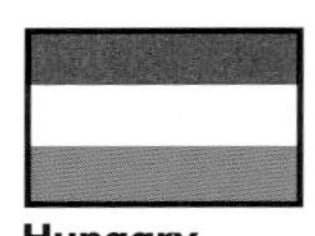
Hungary

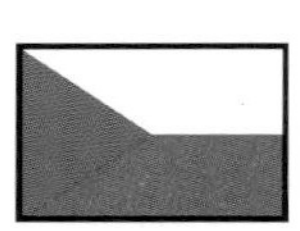
Czech Republic

Slovak Republic

Austria

Germany

Poland

Portugal

Spain

Andorra

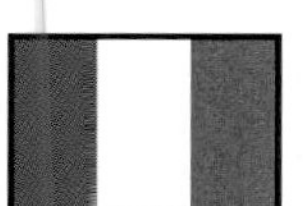
France

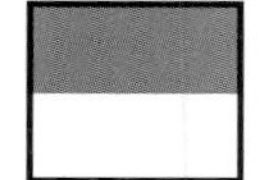
Monaco

Switzerland

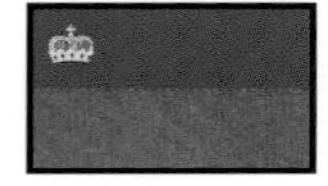
Liechtenstein

AFRICA key facts

Morocco

Mauritius

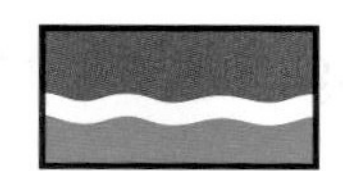
Seychelles

Comoros

Madagascar

Lesotho

South Africa

Namibia

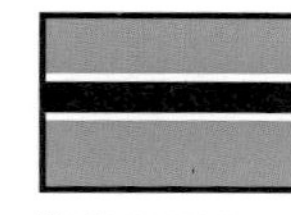
Botswana

Algeria

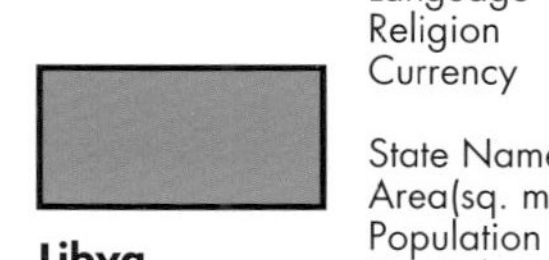
Libya

Egypt

Cape Verde

Mauritania

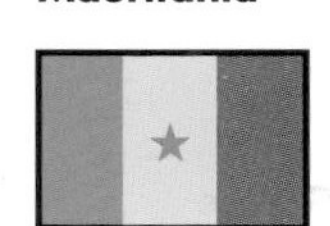
Senegal

Gambia, The

Guinea

Guinea-Bissau

Sierra Leone

Liberia

Ivory Coast

Mali

State Name	Area(sq. miles)	Population	Capital	Language	Religion	Currency
Algeria	919,352	25,360,000	Algiers	Arabic, French	Islam	Algerian dinar
Angola	481,226	10,020,000	Luanda	Portuguese, Tribal	R.C., Tribal	Kwanza
Benin	43,472	4,760,000	Porto-Novo	French, Tribal	Animist	CFA franc
Botswana	224,652	1,260,000	Gaborone	English, Setswana	Tribal, Christian	Pula
Burkina Faso	105,811	8,760,000	Ouagadougou	French, Tribal	Animist, Islam	CFA franc
Burundi	10,744	5,540,000	Bujumbura	French, Kirundi	R.C., Tribal	Burundi franc
Cameroon	183,520	11,540,000	Yaoundé	French, English	Islam, Christian	CFA franc
Cape Verde	1,557	369,000	Praia	Portuguese, Crioulo	Roman Catholic	Cape Verde escudo
C. Af. Rep.	240,260	2,900,000	Bangui	French, Tribal	Animist, Christian	CFA franc
Chad	495,624	5,540,000	N'djaména	French, Arabic	Islam, Animist	CFA franc
Comoros	719	503,000	Moroni	French, Arabic	Islam	Comoran franc
Congo	131,943	2,260,000	Brazzaville	French, Bantu	Animist	CFA franc
Djibouti	8,955	484,000	Djibouti	French, Arabic	Islam	Djibouti franc
Egypt	386,772	50,740,000	Cairo	Arabic	Islam	Egyptian pound
Equat. Guinea	10,827	417,000	Malabo	Spanish, Tribal	Roman Catholic	CFA franc
Eritrea	45,405	3,000,000	Asmara	Arabic, Tigrina	Islam, Christian	Ethiopian birr
Ethiopia	426,248	47,000,000	Addis Ababa	Amharic, Arabic	Islam, Christian	Ethiopian birr
Gabon	103,319	1,220,000	Libreville	French, Tribal	Christian, Tribal	CFA franc
Gambia, The	4,360	875,000	Banjul	English	Islam	Gambian dalasi
Ghana	92,432	14,900,000	Accra	English, Tribal	Christian, Tribal	Cedi
Guinea	94,901	6,710,000	Conakry	French, Tribal	Islam, Animist	Guinea franc
Guinea-Bissau	13,944	966,000	Bissau	Portuguese, Crioulo	Animist, Islam	Peso Guineano
Ivory Coast	124,471	12,100,000	Abidjan	French, Tribal	Tribal, Islam	CFA franc
Kenya	224,884	24,080,000	Nairobi	Kiswahili, English	Christian, Tribal	Kenyan shilling
Lesotho	11,717	1,720,000	Maseru	Sesotho, English	R.C., Protestant	Loti
Liberia	42,989	2,440,000	Monrovia	English, Tribal	Christian, Tribal	Liberian dollar
Libya	679,182	4,000,000	Tripoli	Arabic	Islam	Libyan dinar
Madagascar	226,598	11,440,000	Antananarivo	Malagasy, French	Animist, Christian	Malagasy franc
Malawi	45,708	7,980,000	Lilongwe	English, Chichewa	Animist, Christian	Kwacha
Mali	478,714	9,090,000	Bamako	French, Tribal	Islam, Animist	Mali franc
Mauritania	397,850	1,970,000	Nouakchott	Arabic, French	Islam	Mauritanain ouguiya
Mauritius	787	1,081,669	Port Louis	English, Creole	Hindu, R.C.	Mauritian rupee
Morocco	177,069	24,500,000	Rabat	Arabic, Berber	Islam	Moroccan dirham
Mozambique	308,561	14,900,000	Maputo	Portuguese, Bantu	R.C., Islam	Mozambique metical
Namibia	317,734	1,290,000	Windhoek	English, Afrikaans	Christian, Tribal	S. African rand
Niger	489,062	7,450,000	Niamey	French, Hausa	Islam, Animist	CFA franc
Nigeria	356,576	118,700,000	Abuja	English, Tribal	Christian, Islam	Naira
Rwanda	10,166	6,710,000	Kigali	Kinyarwanda, French	Animist, R.C.	Rwandese franc
São Tomé & P.	386	115,600	São Tomé	Portuguese, Tribal	Roman Catholic	Dobra
Senegal	75,730	7,170,000	Dakar	French, Tribal	Islam	CFA franc
Seychelles	176	67,378	Victoria	Creole, Eng., Fren.	Roman Catholic	Seychelles rupee
Sierra Leone	28,304	4,140,000	Freetown	English, Tribal	Animist, Islam	Leone
Somalia	246,136	6,260,000	Mogadishu	Somali, Arabic	Islam	Somali shilling
South Africa	471,320	30,190,000	Pretoria	Afrikaans, English	R.C., Protestant	S. African rand

Mozambique

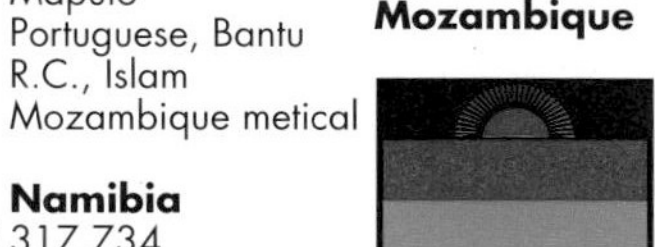
Malawi

Angola

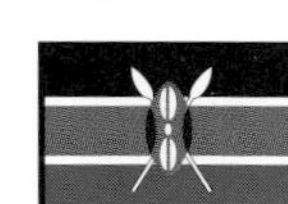
Kenya

Burundi

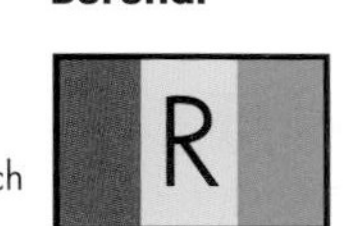
Rwanda

Congo

Gabon

Equat. Guinea

São Tomé & P.

Somalia

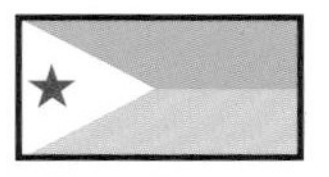
Djibouti

Eritrea

Burkina Faso

Ghana

Benin

Niger

Nigeria

Cameroon

Chad

C. Af. Rep.

Ethiopia

AFRICA/ASIA key facts

Tunisia

Sudan

Swaziland

Zimbabwe

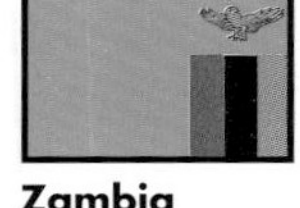
Zambia

Tanzania

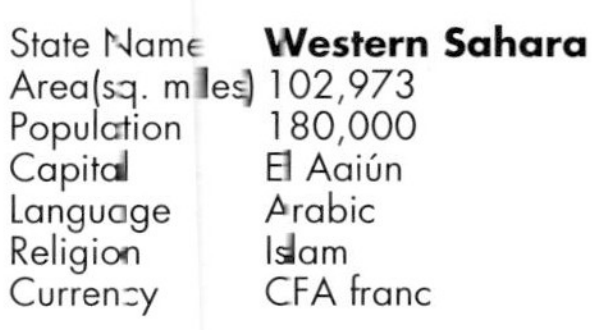

Western Sahara

Uganda

Togo

Zaïre

State Name	Area(sq. miles)	Population	Capital	Language	Religion	Currency
Sudan	967,244	25,560,000	Khartoum	Arabic, Eng., Tribal	Islam, Animist	Sudanese pound
Togo	21,919	3,400,000	Lomé	French, Ewe, Kabre	Animist, R.C., Islam	CFA franc
Western Sahara	102,973	180,000	El Aaiún	Arabic	Islam	CFA franc
Zambia	290,509	8,500,000	Lusaka	English, Tribal	Christian, Animist	Kwacha
Swaziland	6,716	681,059	Mbabane	Swazi, English	Prot., R.C., Animist	Lilangeni
Tunisia	63,362	7,750,000	Tunis	Arabic, French	Islam	Tunisian dinar
Zaïre	905,126	34,140,000	Kinshasa	French, Tribal	R.C., Animist	Zaïre
Zimbabwe	150,833	9,370,000	Harare	English, Tribal	Christian, Animist	Zimbabwe dollar
Tanzania	364,784	24,800,000	Dar es Salaam	Kiswahili, English	Christian, Islam	Tanzanian shilling
Uganda	91,428	17,000,000	Kampala	English, Tribal	R.C., Prot., Animist	Uganda shilling

ASIA

Estonia

Japan

Brunei

Indonesia

Cambodia

Laos

Burma

Latvia

Korea, South

Belarus

Korea, North

Georgia

China

Armenia

Bhutan

Azerbaijan

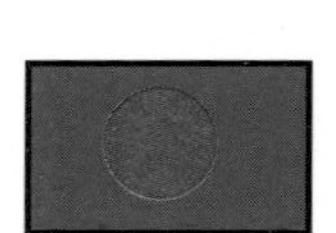
Bangladesh

Kazakhstan

India

Kirghizstan

Afghanistan

State Name	Area(sq. miles)	Population	Capital	Language	Religion	Currency
Afghanistan	251,707	15,810,000	Kabul	Pushtu, Dari	Islam	Afghani
Brunei	2,225	267,000	Bandar Seri Begawan	Malay	Islam	Brunei dollar
Indonesia	740,905	179,100,000	Jakarta	Bahasa Indonesia	Islam	Rupiah
Kirghizstan	76,621	4,300,000	Frunze	Russian, Slavic	Orthodox, Islam	Ruble
Armenia	11,503	3,200,000	Yerevan	Russian, Slavic	Orthodox, Islam	Ruble
Burma	261,159	39,300,000	Rangoon	Burmese	Buddhist	Kyat
Iran	635,128	53 920,000	Tehran	Farsi	Islam	Iranian riyal
Korea, North	46,528	22,420,000	Pyongyang	Korean	Buddhist	Won
Azerbaijan	33,428	7,000,000	Baku	Russian, Slavic	Orthodox, Islam	Ruble
Cambodia	69,880	8,300,000	Phnom Penh	Khmer	Buddhist	Riel
Iraq	167,881	17,060,000	Baghdad	Arabic, Kurdish	Islam	Iraqi dinar
Korea, South	38,300	42,800,000	Seoul	Korean	Budd., Confuc.	Won
Bahrain	262	486,000	Manama	Arabic	Islam	Bahraini dinar
China	3,695,139	1,114,000,000	Beijing	Mandarin Chinese	Confucist, Buddhist	Yuan
Israel	8,017	4,820,000	Jerusalem	Hebrew, Arabic	Jewish, Islam	New Israel shekel
Kuwait	6,878	2,040,000	Kuwait	Arabic	Islam	Kuwati dinar
Bangladesh	55,583	113,340,000	Dhaka	Bengali	Islam	Bangladeshi taka
Estonia	17,409	1,600,000	Tallinn	Estonian, Russian	Orthodox, Lutheran	Ruble
Japan	145,844	123,260,000	Tokyo	Japanese	Buddhist, Shintoist	Japanese yen
Laos	91,405	3,580,000	Vientiane	Laotian	Buddhist	Kip
Belarus	80,134	10,200,000	Minsk	Russian, Slavic	Orthodox, Islam	Ruble
Georgia	26,904	5,500,000	Tbilisi	Georgian, Russian	Orthodox	Ruble
Jordan	35 466	3,170,000	Amman	Arabic	Islam	Jordan dinar
Latvia	24,588	2,700,000	Riga	Latvian, Russian	Orthodox, Lutheran	Ruble
Bhutan	17,949	1,400,000	Thimphu	Dzongkha, Nepali	Buddhist	Ngultrum
India	1,222,396	843,930,000	Delhi	Hindi, English	Hindu, Islam	Rupee
Kazakhstan	1,048,878	16,500,000	Alma-Ata	Russian, Slavic	Orthodox, Islam	Ruble
Lebanon	4,035	2,800,000	Beirut	Arabic	Islam, Christian	Lebanese pound

Lebanon

Israel

Jordan

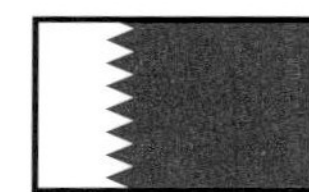
Bahrain

Kuwait

Iraq

Iran

ASIA/OCEANIA key facts

Lithuania

Philippines

Singapore

Malaysia

Vietnam

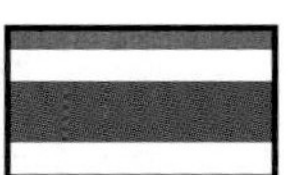
Thailand

Taiwan

Mongolia

Nepal

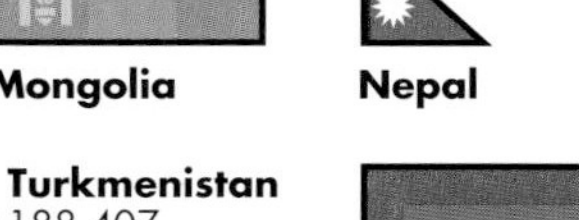

Ukraine

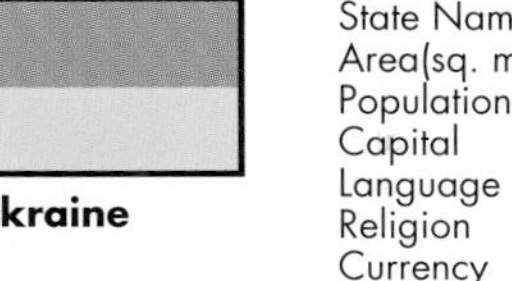

Maldives

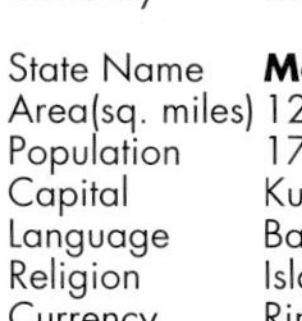
Moldova

Sri Lanka

Russian Fed.

Pakistan

Turkmenistan

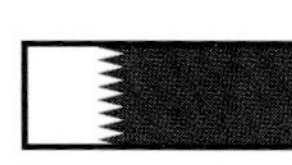
Qatar

Uzbekistan

U.A.E.

Tajikistan

Oman

Turkey

Yemen

Syria

Saudi Arabia

State Name	Area(sq. miles)	Population	Capital	Language	Religion	Currency
Lithuania	25,167	3,700,000	Vilnius	Latvian, Russian	Lutheran, R.C.	Ruble
Pakistan	307,293	105,400,000	Islamabad	Urdu	Islam	Pakistani rupee
Sri Lanka	25,325	16,810,000	Colombo	Sinhala, Tamil	Buddhist, Hindu	Sri Lankan rupee
Turkmenistan	188,407	3,500,000	Ashkhabad	Russian, Slavic	Orthodox, Islam	Ruble
Malaysia	127,287	17,810,000	Kuala Lumpur	Bahasa Malaysia	Islam, Buddhist	Ringgit
Philippines	115,800	60,500,000	Manila	Filipino, English	R.C., Islam	Philippine peso
Syria	71,480	11,300,000	Damascus	Arabic	Islam	Syrian pound
Ukraine	233,028	51,700,000	Kiev	Russian, Slavic	Orthodox, Islam	Ruble
Maldives	115	214,139	Malé	Divehi	Islam	Rufiyaa
Qatar	4,415	371,863	Doha	Arabic	Islam	Qatar riyal
Taiwan	13,963	18,800,000	Taipei	Mandarin Chinese	Buddhist, Confucist	New Taiwan dollar
U.A.E.	32,292	1,600,000	Abu Dhabi	Arabic, English	Islam	U.A.E. dirham
Moldova	13,008	4,300,000	Kishinev	Russian, Slavic	Orthodox, Islam	Ruble
Russian Federation	6,591,104	150,000,000	Moscow	Russian, Slavic	Orthodox, Islam	Ruble
Tajikistan	55,237	5,100,000	Dushanbe	Russian, Slavic	Orthodox, Islam	Ruble
Uzbekistan	172,696	19,900,000	Tashkent	Russian, Slavic	Orthodox, Islam	Ruble
Mongolia	604,862	2,095,000	Ulan Bator	Mongolian	Buddhist	Tugrik
Saudi Arabia	829,780	12,000,000	Riyadh	Arabic	Islam	Saudi Arabian riyal
Thailand	198,062	55,900,000	Bangkok	Thai	Buddhist	Baht
Vietnam	127,213	65,000,000	Hanoi	Vietnamese	Buddhist	Dong
Nepal	56,812	18,000,000	Kathmandu	Nepali, Bihari	Hindu	Nepalese rupee
Singapore	241	2,690,000	Singapore	Chinese, English	Buddhist, Taoist	Singapore dollar
Turkey	300,869	50,670,000	Ankara	Turkish	Islam	Turkish lira
Yemen	204,966	12,000,000	San'a	Arabic	Islam	Yemen riyal
Oman	82,008	2,000,000	Muscat	Arabic	Islam	Omani riyal

OCEANIA

Papua New Guinea

New Zealand

Nauru

Australia

Kiribati

Vanuatu

State Name	Area(sq. miles)	Population	Capital	Language	Religion	Currency
Australia	2,965,368	17,100,000	Canberra	English	Protestant, R.C.	Australian dollar
Nauru	8.2	8,100	Yaren	Nauruan, English	Protestant, R.C.	Australian dollar
Solomon Islands	10,637	308,796	Honiara	English, Tribal	Protestant	Solomon Is. dollar
Vanuatu	4,705	142,630	Vila	Bislama, Eng., Fren.	Christian, Animist	Vatu
Fiji	7,077	727,104	Suva	English, Fijian	Christian, Hindu	Fijian dollar
New Zealand	102,297	3,390,000	Wellington	English, Maori	R.C., Protestant	New Zealand dollar
Tonga	289	95,200	Nuku'alofa	English, Tongan	Protestant, R.C.	Pa'anga
Western Samoa	1,092	163,000	Apia	Samoan, English	Protestant, R.C.	Tala
Kiribati	277	66,250	Tarawa	Kiribati, English	Protestant, R.C.	Australian dollar
Papua New Guinea	178,656	3,800,000	Port Moresby	English, Tribal	Animist, Christian	Kina
Tuvalu	9.5	8,229	Funafuti	Tuvaluan, English	Protestant	Australian dollar

Solomon Islands

Tuvalu

Western Samoa

Tonga

Fiji

THE AMERICAS key facts

Canada

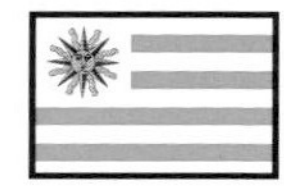
Uruguay

Argentina

Paraguay

Bolivia

Chile

Brazil

U.S.A.

Mexico

Bahamas

Cuba

Jamaica

Haiti

Dominican Republic

Guatemala

Belize

El Salvador

State Name	Area(sq. miles)	Population	Capital	Language	Religion	Currency
Antigua & Barbuda	171	85,000	St John's	English	Protestant	E. Caribbean dollar
Argentina	1,073,116	32,690,000	Buenos Aires	Spanish	Roman Catholic	Austral
Bahamas	5,357	256,000	Nassau	English	Protestant	Bahamian dollar
Barbados	166	260,000	Bridgetown	English	Protestant	Barbados dollar
Belize	8,864	193,000	Belmopan	English, Spanish	Roman Catholic	Belize dollar
Bolivia	424,052	6,400,000	La Paz	Spanish	Roman Catholic	Boliviano peso
Brazil	3,285,619	155,600,000	Brasilia	Portuguese	Roman Catholic	Cruzado
Canada	3,848,655	26,600,000	Ottawa	French, English	Protestant, R.C.	Canadian dollar
Chile	292,180	12,960,000	Santiago	Spanish	Roman Catholic	Chilean peso
Colombia	440,715	33,000,000	Bogotá	Spanish	Roman Catholic	Colombian peso
Costa Rica	19,725	2,910,000	San José	Spanish	Roman Catholic	Costa Rican colón
Cuba	42,792	10,580,000	Havana	Spanish	Roman Catholic	Cuban peso
Dominica	290	81,200	Roseau	English, Creole	Roman Catholic	E. Caribbean dollar
Dominican Rep.	18,699	7,200,000	Santo Domingo	Spanish	Roman Catholic	Dominica peso
Ecuador	109,455	10,490,000	Quito	Spanish, Quecha	Roman Catholic	Sucre
El Salvador	8,258	5,210,000	San Salvador	Spanish	Roman Catholic	Colón
Grenada	133	110,000	St George's	English, French	Roman Catholic	E. Caribbean dollar
Guatemala	42,031	9,000,000	Guatemala City	Spanish	Roman Catholic	Quetzal
Guyana	82,978	990,000	Georgetown	English, Hindi,	Christian, Hindu	Guyana dollar
Haiti	10,712	5,700,000	Port-au-Prince	French, Creole	Roman Catholic	Gourde
Honduras	43,266	4,[illegible]40,000	Tegucigalpa	Spanish	Roman Catholic	Lempira
Jamaica	4,4[illegible]0	2,4[illegible]0,000	Kingston	English	Protestant	Jamaican dollar
Mexico	755,366	81,1[illegible]0,000	Mexico City	Spanish	Roman Catholic	Mexican peso
Nicaragua	49,3[illegible]0	3,750,000	Managua	Spanish	Roman Catholic	Córdoba oro
Panama	29,75[illegible]	2,320,000	Panama City	Spanish, English	Roman Catholic	Balboa
Paraguay	157,0[illegible]2	4,160,[illegible]00	Asunción	Spanish, Guaraní	Roman Catholic	Guaraní
Peru	496,09[illegible]	22.330,000	Lima	Spanish, Quecha	Roman Catholic	Sol
St Kitts-Nevis	101	43,410	Basseterre	English	Protestant	E. Caribbean dollar
St Lucia	238	146,600	Castries	English, French	Roman Catholic	E. Caribbean dollar
St Vincent	150	113,950	Kingstown	English	Protestant R.C.	E. Caribbean dollar
Surinam	63,235	416,839	Paramaribo	Dutch, English	Prot., Hindu, Islam	Surinam guilder
Trinidad & Tobago	1,978	1,240,000	Port-of-Spain	English, Spanish	Christian, Hindu	Trin. & Tob. dollar
U.S.A.	3,617,812	249,630,000	Washington D.C.	English	Protestant, R.C.	U.S. dollar
Uruguay	68,019	3,110,000	Montevideo	Spanish	Roman Catholic	Uruguayan peso
Venezuela	352,051	19,250,000	Caracas	Spanish	Roman Catholic	Bolivár

Peru

Ecuador

Surinam

Guyana

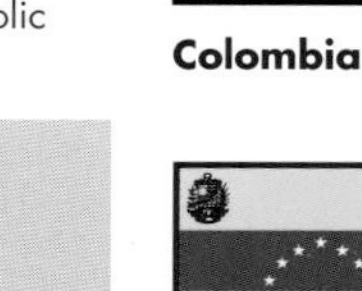
Colombia

Venezuela

Trinidad & Tobago

Grenada

Barbados

St Lucia

Honduras

Nicaragua

Costa Rica

Panama

St Kitts-Nevis

Antigua & Barbuda

Dominica

St Vincent & the Grenadines

GAZETTEER

This section of the book helps you to find the features shown on the maps in the atlas section. The features are listed alphabetically. After the name extra information may be given. For example, "river" after "Amazon". The first number after the listed name refers to the page. The following letter and number refer to the grid square on that page in which the feature can be found. For example, Nouakchott. The index entry reads 28 A3. On page 28 look across the top of the map to the letter A and then down to the number 3. Where these two columns meet Nouakchott can be found.

The following abbreviations have been used in the gazetteer:

P.N.G. – Papua New Guinea
U.A.E. – United Arab Emirates
N.Z. – New Zealand
U.K. – United Kingdom
R.F. – Russian Federation
U.S.A. – United States of America